Handling Church Tensions Creatively

Fred W. Prinzing

HARVEST PUBLICATIONS
Arlington Heights, Illinois 60005

Published by Harvest Publications
Division of the Board of
Educational Ministries
Baptist General Conference
2002 S. Arlington Heights Road
Arlington Heights, IL 60005

ISBN: 0-935797-23-8

DEDICATED TO:

My wife, Anita, and our three children, Debby, Mark and Scott, whose support and encouragement allows me to be a tension adjuster.

ACKNOWLEDGEMENT:

Many people have made helpful suggestions, and to each one I am grateful. First of all, I would like to thank Jim Lemon, who challenged me to write. A special word of appreciation goes to those who have read the manuscript; Harry Buerer, Peggy Larson and Mettie Williams gave valuable comments and insights. Also, I would like to thank my wife, Anita, and the secretaries at Temple Baptist Church, Marianne Goddard and Vicki Gillette, for typing the chapters. Finally, I want to thank the Church Staff at Temple Baptist Church of Portland for assuming extra responsibilities during this writing project.

TABLE OF CONTENTS

FOREWORD

Two casts, two strikes, two lost Alaskan salmon. I'd paid careful attention to everything...except the tension. With the drag on the reel too tight, the salmon struck and took the lure with them. The rod was adequate for the task, the reel and line had the potential to do the job...I just neglected a minor detail...and lost the fish. A simple adjustment changed the odds in my favor.

Through twenty-five years of ministry, Dr. Fred Prinzing has paid attention to the tension. He's lost a few fish and learned at the same time. If you've ever struggled with tension, believe me, his insights will help you process it productively. Tension can be an enemy...or a friend. It can build momentum towards success or failure.

Life and ministry involve all kinds of people, with their unique perceptions, their concerns, their problems. Diversity of opinion and varying cultural and religious traditions make tension inevitable. It's here to stay, and it can be a friend. Dr. Prinzing selects twelve familiar ministry-related tensions and helps the reader understand the issues and move towards their resolution. His years of ministry experience are readily apparent.

Personal illustrations abound. At times he charges in where angels fear to tread, and confronts sacred cows, cultural traditions and touchy subjects with discretion, balance and a touch of humor. My only regret is that Dr. Prinzing waited until now to write his book. My seven years in the pastorate would have been more productive and less stressful if I'd understood the ideas discussed in his important work. It should be required reading for every prospective or full-time minister, as well as every church board member.

Ministries will be enriched and church leaders encouraged through Dr. Prinzing's insights into the perils and possibilities of tension management. If your drag is too tight, your line is breaking and the fish are getting away, this book is for you.

Joseph C. Aldrich
President of Multnomah School of the Bible

Introduction

"Tension — Good or Bad?"

"They don't understand *us,"* one of the deacons said as he dug his index finger into my chest. *"You* will understand what I mean after you are here awhile."

This was my introduction to the subject of tension in the local church. I was twenty-six years old and this was my first church pastorate after graduating from seminary. To say I was still wet behind the ears would be putting it mildly. Maybe a better way to describe my naivete would be to say that I had "three degrees and no temperature."

My desire was to serve the Lord and His people. I assumed that no matter what differences my new friends and I would have, we would subordinate them as we served God together.

I wondered what the deacon meant by separating all people into three categories — *they, us* and *you?* I didn't understand, but it didn't take me long to find out about these distinctions. *They* represented the people from the denominational office in the big city of Chicago. Although they were supposed to be helping us start a church, they didn't know anything about rural people, rural life, or rural problems. Because they were far away, they could be mistaken at worst as the enemies and at best as strangers.

Us included all the people who were born and raised in the rural community where the church was located. The church met in the town hall of a township of 1,600 people, who lived within 36 square miles. The people had their own set of standards, their own moral code and their own educational requirements. Very few of them had ever graduated from high school. Most of them had large gardens and raised a few animals. The nearest city was 8 to 10 miles away.

I was referred to as *you,* and did not belong to either of the previous groups. Not only was I young and overly educated, but I talked and dressed differently than 'us.' For instance, I wore a hat, to keep from catching cold in the winter and getting sunburn in the summer. And I wore a topcoat in the winter, a sign to them that I wasn't tough enough. They would tolerate me because of my position as the pastor of the church, but the jury would remain out, deciding whether or not they were going to accept me as a person into their group.

Despite this uncertainty over the question of my acceptance, I decided to work hard, love the people and try to eliminate any problems. Whenever there was a conflict or tension, I would immediately jump into my car and attempt to extinguish the fire. But I had no idea how to prevent the fire. During the first several months I put many miles on my car acting as a "fire fighter." The tensions and conflicts continued to increase until my second year, when they finally came to a head.

The Monday Night Hat Massacre

The congregation had purchased three acres of land for a

building site across the street from where we were meeting. The purchase price was $300 and some questioned the wisdom of spending that much money. We decided to build the church with volunteer labor so we could save as much money as possible. Before we could begin to build, the property needed to be cleared of all the shrubs and trees.

Several nights were scheduled for the men to get the property cleared. On one hot, humid summer evening, I borrowed an ax and showed up ready to work with my new straw hat sitting proudly on my head. Even though I knew very little about clearing property, I was sure that everyone would appreciate my willingness to become involved.

There was quite a crew that night and we worked hard and long. As it began to get dark, we decided to call it quits. Some of the ladies had arrived at the town hall with refreshments. My spirits were high. The church was growing, and we were now starting a building program. On the surface it appeared that I was working well with the people toward mutual goals. As I sat enjoying my lemonade, I noticed several of the men coming across the street. They were absorbed in intense discussion.

As they approached me, one of the men grabbed my straw hat. I was stunned. My immediate reaction was to do nothing. There seemed to be only two alternatives: get my hat back, or grab his. (I could see the headline of the local newspaper: "Pastor and Deacon Get in Brawl Over Hats".) The men took my hat and placed it on the ground and stood in a circle around it. After exchanging glances, they started swinging their axes, cutting my hat into shreds. For a few moments we all stood in silence as the darkness began to cover us.

The next sounds I can remember hearing were the turning of ignitions and the shifting of gears as the men began to drive away. I stood alone. In my condition, it was a good thing that no one else was there. Solitude was a welcome friend. When

I was sure that everyone was gone, I put the remains of my hat into the car, drove home and threw what was left of it into the incinerator in my back yard.

I can't remember what happened during the rest of the evening. Perhaps I was too embarrassed or too bewildered to tell Anita about the incident. I couldn't sleep. My mind was in overdrive and my body shifting gears quite often. Unanswered questions kept rising up before me. Why were the men so disrespectful? What had I done to precipitate the Monday night massacre of my hat? Should I leave this church? Should I leave the ministry? All of the air was let out of my balloon. One of the conclusions that I came to that evening was that my effectiveness as a leader, at least at that church, had been severely damaged. The question I couldn't answer was, "Had it been damaged beyond repair?"

The next day one of the men who had been involved in "the hat incident" called to express his regrets for his part in the previous night's activities. Before he hung up, he said that he felt so badly about the occurrence that he had opened an account at the finest men's store in town so that I could buy a new hat. (I never took him up on his offer.) After the church service the next Sunday, another one of the men said that he wanted to talk to me. He apologized for his actions and added, "From now on *we* are 100% behind *you*, Pastor."

Little did I realize that the "hat incident" was going to be a turning point, not only in my ministry at this little church but in the future as well. My perceived "defeat" was the beginning of a new chapter in my ministry. From that point on I began to feel accepted. Although they still referred to the denominational leaders in the big city as *they*, I was not referred to as *you*. The three categories of *they, you* and *us*, were reduced to two — *they* and *us*.

As I related the story to other people through the years, many asked me why the men had destroyed my hat. Although

I had asked myself the same question, I never was able to come up with an adequate answer. Years later I was invited to speak at the tenth anniversary of the founding of the church. By then the "story of the preacher's hat" had become a bit of a legend in the community. Each time the incident was related, everyone got a good laugh. I took the opportunity to ask one of the men who had stood in the circle and cut up my hat, why they had done it.

He said that for many years there were threshing crews that traveled up from the South to Michigan at harvest time. Any time there was a "rookie" on the crew, they would grab his hat and throw it through the threshing machine. Their action was an initiation rite.

None of us at the time understood the significance of the "hat incident." Even from the very beginning of our relationship as pastor and people, I had never experienced any real conflict. However, there was an underlying tension that I failed to recognize. There were differences not only between us, but among them. Some of the obvious differences were our ages, our education, our appearance and our geographic locations. These differences were not right or wrong, but they had an impact on our personalities, our philosophies, our priorities and our values.

Following the hat incident, I was determined to learn how to prevent as many conflicts and ease as many tensions as I could. After 25 years in the ministry, serving churches on the East coast, West coast and Midwest, I have begun to gain some insights into the subject. I learned how to analyze a congregation, whether it was rural, urban, or suburban. Losing a hat was not that important. There were other things that could be more valuable if I were to lose them.

Tension: Constructive or Destructive?

Tension in the local church: Is it good or is it bad? Is it inevitable? Should all tensions and conflicts be eliminated from churches?

Someone has said that there are three certain things in life: taxes, death and tension in churches. The usual connotation of the word tension is a negative one. People have "tension headaches." When you walk into a room "filled with tension," it is not a pleasant experience. Tension, however, is not necessarily bad. In fact, a lack of tension in many situations could be disastrous, if not fatal.

It is important to define what I mean by tension and how it differs from conflict. Tension is the "stretching of two opposite forces while searching for a proper balance." Tension is neither good nor bad. But our responses to tension can be either constructive or destructive. In every area of life we must learn creative and positive ways to adjust tension.

For instance, on a sewing machine there is a knob called a "tension adjuster." This regulates the amount of tension put on the thread as it stitches the cloth. You either loosen or tighten the tension, depending upon the fabric. Sometimes the stitches are so tight that they will snap when any stress is put on the seam; other times the stitches are so loose that they barely hold the seam together. A skilled seamstress will understand the existence and the purpose of the tension. She will understand that the finished product will not be usable unless the tension is properly adjusted.

Not only is skill needed in learning how to adjust tension as you work with fabric, but also in other areas, such as sports. For instance, a successful fisherman has learned the art of adjusting tension. There is tremendous tension created between a fisherman and a salmon. They are pulling in opposite directions on a thin nylon line. What enables the angler to land the salmon is his knowledge and use of tension. If the line is too loose, the fish will never be reeled in. On the other hand, if the tension is too tight, the line will snap. On the reel there is a little knob that enables the fisherman to apply just the right amount of tension. How to apply the tension depends on the type of fishing, the type of water and the type of line used. Without tension the fisherman cannot catch fish.

Adjusting Tensions in the Church

In a church you are not dealing with machines or fish, but with people. Even so, the process of adjusting tensions is the same for us. The existence of tension is a sign of life. When tension ceases to exist, so does the vitality of the church. Our efforts in a local church must not be to eliminate tension, but to creatively adjust it so that the church can function properly in order to fulfill its purpose.

Tension adjustment deals with preventing conflict rather than with handling problems after they arise. In a church there are both tensions and conflicts. A wise leader will learn the difference between the two. A conflict is a struggle between competitive and incompatible ideas, interests and individuals. Tensions emphasize stretching, growth, health and balance. Conflicts emphasize confrontation, friction and competition. A proper use of tension prevents problems before they occur, while conflicts deal with problems that already exist. Tensions can potentially turn into conflicts when several conditions exist.

1. When the church does not have a clear purpose and goals
2. When people do not desire biblical unity
3. When tension is viewed as an enemy
4. When the causes of tension are not understood

5. When tensions are seen as competitive, not complimentary
6. When one of the forces causing the tension is not biblical

There has been a great deal written in recent years about "conflict management" in the church. Although most of us avoid dealing with conflict, we need to face it when it occurs. We need skilled "conflict managers" in our churches.

This book, however, is not another book about conflict management. Its purpose is to help us become "tension adjusters." The emphasis is placed on preventing tensions from becoming conflicts and confrontations. The following chapters focus on twelve common tensions which, if improperly adjusted, can sap the spiritual vitality of your church. In each chapter, and in the concluding chapter, you'll find specific steps your church can take to become skilled tension adjusters in these and other situations.

1

The Brown Envelope or the White Envelope?

The Tension Between Home and World Missions

My parents were faithful church members. Not only did they believe that it was important to attend church, but also to extend the church. For them the main purpose of the church was to reach the world for Jesus Christ. All other functions of the church were secondary. Not only was foreign missions preached from the pulpit, but my parents gave sacrificially.

My parents gave me seven cents each Saturday. The entire amount was to go to church. I never was tempted to spend the money on something else because I got an allowance every week in addition to the seven cents. The problem with the seven cents — a nickel and two pennies — was that I had to decide where to put the money.

At the beginning of Sunday school class each week the teacher passed around two envelopes. The only difference between the two was that one was white and the other was brown. All of us knew that. The white envelope was for general expense (whatever that was), and the brown one was for missions. Our teachers never tried to persuade us to give to one or the other. There was no way to divide seven cents into two equal amounts. The decision that I had to make as a Sunday school student was to become a lifelong tension. In fact, the two envelopes represented groups in the church. One group saw the church as merely the agency where resources were provided and personnel were challenged to reach a dying world for Christ. The other group was concerned about Sunday school classes and youth groups that would provide spiritual training for their children. The dichotomy was not a surface distinction. It usually was based on a deep, underlying conviction. There were some people in the church who believed that those who supported missions — which was a term that was synonymous with foreign missions — were spiritual. Those who didn't were materialistic at best and worldly at worst.

On the other hand, there were those who believed that if God wanted people on the other side of the world to hear about Christ, He would make sure they heard. Our responsibility was to provide for our own family and our own community. Quite often this tension came to a conflict at budget time when the Trustee Board (they had the responsibility to pay the bills) and the Mission Committee fought over the allocation of the same dollar. The policy of the church that 50 percent of the total giving goes to missions was always open to challenge.

My family was definitely on the side of missions. I'm sure that this was one of the reasons why I put my seven cents into the brown envelope. I also found a great deal of satisfaction in realizing that I was helping the heathen come to Christ.

One Envelope, But Still a Decision

Probably no church uses the white and brown envelope system anymore. Most churches have only one envelope. The tension is no longer simply between missions and the general fund. It's much more complicated. On most envelopes there are several options for people to designate their giving: General Expenses, Missions, Building Fund, Scholarship Fund, or a Special Project.

There are still some people who do not believe in or support missions. This group in most evangelical churches represents a small minority. In most churches the tension involves missions supporters. Do we support missions "over there" or "right here"? Is the church's missionary emphasis going to be to reach the people without Christ who live "overseas" or the people without Christ who live in "our neighborhood"? It's a tension between "home" and "foreign," or between "here" and "there."

During World War I my uncle and aunt had wanted to go to Africa as missionaries. They applied and were turned down by a mission society, for health reasons. Instead of accepting the verdict as final, it made them more determined than ever to go. They had heard God's call and knew they must obey. Since there was no agency to send them out, our family assumed the responsibility. The mission board consisted of family members plus a few interested pastors and laymen. My father was the treasurer, my mother was the secretary and my grandfather, who lived in our home, was the executive secretary.

Most of the missionaries were family members — uncles, aunts and cousins. My oldest sister felt a call to be a missionary to Africa. There were not any alternatives. She felt so strongly about her call from God that when she attended a Christian college she would not date anyone who wasn't planning to be a missionary to Africa. This limited her selection considerably. You guessed it! She met a young man who also was planning to be a missionary to Africa and they got married. Along with other couples and singles from our church, they were young people that everyone admired and respected. It seemed that God was calling the best.

Over a period of a couple of decades our church sent out twenty missionaries. When we sent missionaries to another country, they became "heroes of the faith." While they were gone, everyone attentively read or listened to the missionary letters. Anticipation increased several months before the missionary was to return for a well deserved furlough. Furloughs were rather infrequent. Usually they occurred every five years. Sometimes, when a replacement was not available, it might be ten years before the missionary returned home.

All of the missionaries we supported were well known to the congregation. Most of them were members of our local church. The highlight of the year was the Sunday that the missionary spoke and showed his or her slides. In many churches there was probably no person higher on the proverbial "spiritual ladder" of importance than the missionary. If God called someone to be a missionary, it was for life. There was no distinction between career missionary and short-term missionary. Being a missionary was like being married. There was no period of time for people to see whether or not they would like being a missionary. It was for keeps. Only a missionary's death or the death of a spouse was a legitimate reason for a missionary to come home.

The only kind of missionaries we knew were "foreign missionaries." Occasionally we were introduced to people who worked with "mountain people" in our country. They were different than people who went overseas. Our emphasis was quite often on the place you were going, not the people you were reaching. Mission organizations had places in their names like "China," "Africa" and "Congo."

There were three messages that were emphasized continually from the pulpit and in Sunday school classes. The first message was that people who were not Christians were lost. Although the question, "Are the heathen lost?" was quite often a topic of discussion, the teaching of the church was that unless they believed in Christ, they were lost. Matthew 28:18-20 was the church's mandate. Everyone knew the Great Commission.

A second message included in the Great Commission was that Christians were "to go" to tell the heathen about Christ. If you were not someone that God had chosen to go, you were responsible to send and support those who had decided to go. "Going" meant "overseas." Wherever it was that you were going, you needed to take a boat to get there. The world was across the ocean. Being a missionary meant being sent to a place other than where you were.

The third message was one of priority. There was an urgency in the Great Commission. Heathen were dying who had never heard. Christ was coming soon. Doors of opportunity to many countries were closing. No one had the right to hear the gospel twice before everyone had heard it once. Because of the number of churches in this country, the abundance of literature available, and the number of preachers on the radio, it was assumed everyone here had heard the gospel message.

The urgency of sharing the gospel with people who lived someplace else was the message of the church. Whether a church could be considered successful or not was determined by how they could answer key questions. How many people did your church send out as "foreign missionaries?" What was the size of your missionary budget? The goal for many churches was to give 50 percent of the total giving to missions. Whether a church was considered missionary-minded or not depended upon how its members were able to answer these questions.

Although there were foreigners in our community, they usually didn't look any different. They were considered foreigners if they didn't speak English. All of the foreigners in our area were European immigrants, except the family who ran the Chinese laundry. Few of the people were recent immigrants. Their families had come from Europe in the late 18th and early 19th centuries. Because my family also had come from the same place, we would not consider our neighbors as either "heathen" or "foreign."

Changes in Our World

Two changes happened after World War II which radically altered many people's view of missions, including mine. One change was that there was a population shift within this country. People who had lived in the same house, attended the same school and worshiped at the same church, got the urge to move. The mobility rate increased rapidly. People were moving from the South to the North, and from the country to the city, and from the city to the suburbs. Quite often people moved because of unemployment, inadequate housing, inferior education and too much crime. Most of the population shifts, except for black people, brought new people who were quite similar racially and ethnically to our communities. Differences were more financial, educational and cultural.

There was another change that was greatly to affect the Christian view of missions. New immigration patterns were emerging. Before 1960, most of the immigrants had come from Europe and Canada. In fact, between 1940 and 1960, 70 percent of all immigrants had come from these countries. Since 1960, less than 30 percent have come from these parts of the world.

The first wave of new immigrants came from Latin America, Asia and Africa. Another wave came in the late 1970s. Many people were forced by war and poverty to leave the shores of Southeast Asia. Following this wave, tremendous numbers of refugees came from the Caribbean and Central America. Because of the various Immigration Acts, the number of newcomers per year in the 1980s increased to new levels in our country. Not since the 1920s had we seen so many new faces.[1]

Not only did legal immigration increase in record numbers, but so did illegal immigration. Although it is not possible to accurately count the number of "invisible immigrants" who illegally enter this country yearly, it is estimated that there are between 3.5 million and 6 million. Most of these are Hispanics from south of the border.[2]

Another change in the immigration pattern has been the rising tide of students coming to schools in this country. Twenty years ago there were fewer than 100,000 international students in the U.S. By 1985 the number had risen to over 500,000 from over 200 countries.[3] Not only were these students from many places, but many students represented the sharpest minds in their countries. Some became leaders in their countries after returning home. The only exposure to Christianity that many of them had was during their student years in America.

The world has drastically changed. People who once were "over there" have come "right here." America is now the fifth largest mission field in the world. It has become a microcosm of the world. Children in the Los Angeles school system speak 104 languages. L.A. is the second largest Korean city in the world. Chicago is the second largest Polish city in the world. Miami has the second largest Cuban population and New York the second largest Puerto Rican population.

Besides ethnic diversity, there is a tremendous religious diversity in the United States. It is estimated that there are 27 million cultists, 6 million Jews, 3 million Muslims and 2.4 million Hindus.

It is apparent that missions no longer can be viewed from a strictly geographic viewpoint. *Places* are still important, but *people* are more important. A mission philosophy that is based on the idea that people must "go" to be involved in the missionary enterprise is only seeing part of the picture. The emphasis needs to be placed on reaching "unreached people" no matter where they are.

Getting a Larger View of Missions

A complete picture of missions in the local church includes the Great Commission as taught in Matthew 28:18-20. Jesus gave orders in anthropological terms. The participles are "go," "baptize" and "teach." The imperative is to make "disciples of all nations." In the Greek, the word for nations is *ethne*, from which we get our English word ethnic. Our environment is becoming more and more ethnic.

As our community changes, our churches ought to reflect the multi-ethnic world community and affect it with the gospel. In Acts 1:8, there is both a geographic emphasis and a strategic emphasis. The responsibility to be witnesses not only includes the "end of the earth," but Jerusalem, Judea and Samaria as well. When the Jews heard the last words of Jesus in Acts 1:8, they had no trouble understanding where Jesus was asking them to go and what He has asked them to do. The imperative was to be "witnesses," wherever they were.

The early Christians were reluctant to share their faith, just as we are today. It is not easy to witness to those who are antagonistic and unreceptive. In Acts 8:1 we read that it took a great persecution against the church in Jerusalem before they were scattered throughout Judea and Samaria. Today, a twentieth century understanding of our Judeas and Samarias and the ends of the earth would include not only a place, but a people.

In past years, people who hadn't heard the gospel were not only culturally removed but also geographically removed. People who were black lived with people who were black. People who were yellow lived with people who were yellow. People who were red lived with people who were red. People who were white lived with people who were white. When Acts 1:8 was written, people who were white, for example, were the people who lived in the "ends of the earth." As we try to understand that verse in America today, many of us see ourselves as living in Jerusalem, and those who are white are at the "center of the earth."

The Great Commission was given almost 2,000 years ago. It has never changed. Jesus' last words cannot be altered or eliminated. It is up to us to obey them and determine how to apply them in our geographical and cultural settings.

The second half of this commandment cannot be understood until there first of all has been a commitment to the Lordship of Jesus Christ. Loving people whom I don't know is much easier than loving my neighbors. When my neighbors happen to be different racially, ethnically and culturally, this is the acid test. Our desire to reach people in another country should not be any different than to reach the same people who move to our country, if that desire is motivated by the same love. It is not a conditional or limited love.

Reconciliation of God to man is communicated both by words and through relationships. In 2 Corinthians 5:18,19 we read, "All this is from God, who reconciled us to himself through Christ and gave us the *ministry* of reconciliation. . . . And he has committed to us the *message* of reconciliation." The pattern of the early church was one that included both of these elements. In Acts 8, an Ethiopian was reading Isaiah 53. God commanded Philip to go and tell him the good news. The truth comes from both Isaiah 53 and from Philip's obedient action. Both the message of reconciliation and the ministry of reconciliation are essential to the communication of the gospel.

Our love, expressed in the Great Commandment, and our obedience, expressed in the Great Commission, is finally placed alongside our involvement, expressed in the Great Compassion. In Mark 6:34, "When Jesus landed and saw a large crowd, he had compassion on them, because they were like sheep without a shepherd." Compassion is different than pity. Pity denotes "feeling sorry" for a person's condition. On the other hand, compassion is an action word which includes the willingness to do something about the person's condition. In the parable of the Good Samaritan, the Priest and the Levite expressed pity, but the Good Samaritan by doing something about the man's condition, showed compassion.

Causes of the Tension

In a local church, the tension between home and foreign, or the here and there, is usually caused by an overemphasis or a neglect of one of the three parts of the gospel message — the Great Commission, the Great Commandment or the Great Compassion. For instance, there are people who believe that their entire effort must be directed toward getting the message of the gospel to people in other places around the world.

Then there are those who believe that we have a priority responsibility to the lost in our own country. Some of these are against foreign missions, period, while others believe that sending out missionaries is not an efficient way to do things today. They contend that training missionary candidates is too costly and time consuming. And they point to the drop-out rate of those who eventually do go as alarming. The detractors of the present foreign mission program believe that money, if it is to be spent on people, should be spent on training indigenous church leaders. Others believe that new means of communication such as the satellite make other methods inefficient and obsolete.

On the other hand, there are people who believe we should support those who go and we should love people around the world, but they are unwilling to get involved with people within their own sphere of influence. Some of the views that Christians have regarding missions are the result of disobedience to God's clear teaching about the subject. Others have belief systems that are based on blind spots or on an overemphasis on certain aspects of missions.

A proper balance of missions is something that is done both "here" and "there." You need to see the mission of your church from a world perspective. Our task is to disciple *all* nations, whether these people live across the ocean or across the street. Foreign and home missions are not in competition. They are part of the same mission of the church. Methods may change from one country and one culture to another, but our priority is to disciple people.

The task of tension adjusting in the church is to keep the tension between "here" and "there" in balance. A strong local church that has no vision for the people of the world is neglecting an essential part of the Great Commission. Conversely, those who have a strong emphasis on world missions, but no vision for their own community, are neglecting an essential part of the Great Commission. Ruth Siemens, a staff worker for Inter-Varsity Christian Fellowship, states in an article entitled "Getting God's Global Perspective," that "Soldiers who do not care about other fronts have not understood what the war is all about and cannot therefore see even their immediate work right."[4]

Before adjusting the tension between "here" and "there" in a local church, it is necessary to understand the causes of the tension. Part of the cause is disobedience. Other causes relate to yesterday's mission mindset, which emphasized places rather than people.

What are the two biggest problems that churches face in helping people become world Christians? They are the same two problems found in other areas of church life. Someone decided to go door to door and take a survey. There was one question on the survey. It was, "What is the biggest problem in the church today, *ignorance* or *apathy?*" One man's answer was quite concise: "I don't know; I don't care." Ignorance and apathy play a strong part in raising tensions in a church's mission strategy.

Three Responses to This Tension

How do you adjust the tension in the church between foreign and home missions? There are no easy solutions. It is a process that should include three responses to the cross-cultural challenge that faces the church body.

A. *Cross-Cultural Education*

Missions education in local churches often is done haphazardly, if at all. Outside of an occasional missionary speaker or the annual mission week, there is little effort given to missions education. A good place to start is for someone in the church to be assigned to be a mission-teacher-at-large. This person may be a former missionary or someone who has had cross-cultural experience. The purpose of this person is to raise the students' awareness about the peoples of the world. On an adult level there may be a class taught for a quarter every year on this subject.

Students who have an interest in cross-cultural ministry can be encouraged to attend mission conferences, such as Urbana. Prayer support and communication can be maintained through letters to people from other cultures. Subscriptions to such magazines as *World Christian* can be sent to interested students.

When my wife and I have traveled to other countries, we were amazed at how many people know more than one language. Many helps are available to assist people in learning another language. Both young people and adults can be encouraged to learn another language, particularly one they can put to use. The church also can be a part of an exchange program where young people can take a year of their education in another country. "Christians cannot afford the luxury of only one language even if they never go overseas."[5]

B. *Cross-Cultural Exposure*

When my brothers were growing up in a Chicago suburb, they didn't travel more than 200 miles away from home. After my sister went to Africa to be a missionary and my brothers served in World War II, there was a big difference in their lives. One brother went to Europe. The other to Asia. Traveling to other continents is no longer limited to missionaries and military personnel. It is a way of life. I encourage your family to include cross-cultural exposure in your vacation plans. Contact missionary organizations and personnel before your visit.

Cross-cultural exposure is not limited to those who have the money or the time to travel. It is important that you and others in your church understand your "backyard" accessibility to cross-cultural people. Make a study of your community or nearby community to discover "target groups" of people. Every church can consider adopting a refugee family or an ethnic church within its own geographic area.

Also, there are wonderful opportunities available to you if you live near a school that enrolls international students. Invite students to your home and volunteer to drive them to see your area. These are ways to minister to them as well as to learn from them. One couple in our church, while still in their eighties, went each week aboard foreign ships docked in Portland harbor and bring wholesome reading material to sailors from other countries. They have the freedom to present the gospel. Each church, no matter where it is located, can find creative ways to expose its members to cross-cultural opportunities.

C. *Cross-Cultural Experiences*

Missionary work requires both career and short-term candidates. Many of the workers who volunteered to go overseas after World War II are now approaching retirement. Replacements are desperately needed. It's important for your pastor and missions committee to encourage you and others to consider your response to the need to prepare yourselves to be missionaries.

Your church may be able to provide "short-term" missionary experiences for your members. People from youth through retirement years can consider serving from three months up to two years in missionary service. Summer Mission Projects to other countries, such as Mexico, or to ethnic churches in large cities are ways that you can get involved in short-term cross-cultural experiences.

Some people can serve as tutors for those who are trying to learn English as a second language. There is a growing need for people with TESL skills to serve in this way. Your church could consider hiring a missionary to serve in your community. When a particular mission field has closed, a missionary can often be brought back home to serve alongside of others with the same kind of ethnic group. A national from another country can be brought to this country to serve his people who have moved here.

We need to be aware of people, programs and periodicals that will assist us in adjusting this tension in our churches. God expects us to be reaping in our own harvest field before we assist in the work of another field.

Footnotes
1.   *Time*, July 8, 1985, Time, Inc. Los Angeles, CA, pp. 34, 35.

2.   *Time, ibid.*

3.   *Christianity Today*, July 12, 1985, p. 20.

4.   Siemens, Ruth, *The Great Commission Handbook* (Evanston IL: Sherman Marketing Services, 1984), p. 70.

5.   *Ibid.* Ruth Siemens, p. 70.

2

Our Kind of People

The Tension Between Uniformity and Diversity

I grew up in the protected world of a Chicago suburb. Although it was not exclusive by design, all the people were the same kind as my family. There were some ethnic differences, but the vast majority of people who lived in my neighborhood were white (from Europe) Protestants, middle-class and working-class. Today we would be called a WASP neighborhood (White Anglo-Saxon Protestant). I can't recall any Jewish people who lived in our neighborhood, and the few Roman Catholic families I knew were the outsiders.

The schools I attended and the church where I worshiped reflected my community. If we knew people who were different, we didn't socialize or worship with them. Our philosophy was one that my mother taught me, "Birds of a feather flock together." We believed that although God wanted us to respect "other kinds" of people, He wanted us to associate with our kind. In some communities the differences between race and religion were even more pronounced. Dr. A. W. Criswell, pastor of the First Baptist Church of Dallas, Texas, described the place where he grew up. He said, "In our community there were two churches — the Baptist Church and the Methodist Church. We learned to love God and hate the Methodists."

It was years later that I discovered the other half of the truth that "birds of a feather flock together." There was a sign on a church bulletin board which stated, "We shall be judged by the people we keep away from." What should my attitude be about people who are different? What kind of relationship should I have with those who are not my kind of people?

My schooling and work opportunities took me to different areas of the country. While in seminary, and also in my first pastorate, I found myself in rural communities where all the people were quite similar in their backgrounds.

When I was 30 years old I moved to a completely different setting. My new home was on the East Coast and my job took me into the metropolitan New York City area. I was responsible for starting new churches. Initially, I and others would survey the area to determine if the elements were favorable for starting a new church. We evaluated elements such as the number of existing churches, proximity to evangelical churches, number of unchurched people and the religious, social, ethnic and economic makeup of the community.

While traveling near a housing development in New York City, a pastor-friend of mine mentioned that this was an area with several thousand people living in it and there wasn't one church. "Why don't we start a church there?" I asked excitedly. "We could never start a church there," he replied, "they are not our kind of people." The people who lived there were upper-class Jewish people. In other communities the population was 80 percent to 90 percent Roman Catholic.

It was difficult to start churches in areas where people's race, religion or national origin differed from the group I represented.

These people were not "our kind of people," but we sent missionaries to other places to start churches among the kinds of people that differed from us. Granted it was not easy to start a church among people who were different, but was it biblical? The question stuck in my mind, "Are our kind of people God's kind of people?" I could not escape the basic truth found in Matthew 1:21, ". . . and you are to give him the name Jesus, because he will save *his people* from their sins." Were *my kind* of people and *His kind* of people the same?

Conformity or Diversity?

On the surface the problem appears to be a racial and religious one. The tension that we need to face is much deeper. When you deal with the subject of similarities and differences among people, you are dealing with the basic tension between homogeneity and heterogeneity. A homogeneous group of people is a group of people who consider themselves to be "our kind of people." They share the same culture and many areas of mutual interest. They are comfortable with each other and socialize easily. Proponents of the homogeneous unit principle believe that churches grow best when they consist of the same kind of people.

Those who support heterogeneity in the church believe that the very nature of the church demands that it include different kinds of people. Although they admit that people will worship and grow where they feel most comfortable, the church, they believe, has a responsibility to seek unity through diversity. The church is to be different than society. Churches are not simply to reflect society, but to help shape it.

Most churches will say that their doors are open to everybody. Everyone is welcome, no one is excluded! Exclusion is perhaps too strong a word. It gives the image of someone standing at the door forbidding people to enter or kicking them out after they are discovered to be different. A better description of the current situation in churches is that there are people who feel they are not welcome. Although philosophically everyone is welcome, in reality they are not.

Lyle Schaller in *The Parish Paper* has an article that deals with the subject, "Whom do you exclude?"[1] He lists many kinds of people who do not feel welcome in most churches. In order to understand the tension between homogeneity and heterogeneity in the church, we first need to look at the broad picture. Let us examine how widespread the practice of exclusion has become in many churches.

Racial Diversity

When most of us think of the tension regarding "our kind" of people, we think of racial differences. Most of the early immigrants to the U.S. were European. Many were not welcome. This was also true of black people and American Indians. With the new immigration to this country following World War II, many other people such as the Hispanics, Southeast Asians and those from the Caribbean joined those who did not feel welcome.

There were several solutions proposed to solve this obvious injustice. Perhaps the major emphasis following World War II was the push for integration. Churches were encouraged to become leaders in breaking down the barriers of racism, ageism and sexism. The U.S. government gave impetus to this approach during the civil rights debate of the 1960s. Whether or not attempts to integrate churches have succeeded or failed is still subject to debate. The fact remains that there are few integrated churches.

Segregation was not confined to any region of America, but was consciously or unconsciously operating in churches in every area of the country. I asked a black pastor in Portland, Oregon how many integrated churches there were in Portland. He replied, "There are many biracial churches in Portland, but just a couple of integrated churches." Because people sit and rub elbows in the same pew during a worship service with someone of another race does not make a church integrated.

America was supposed to be the place where people would feel that they were welcome, especially in churches. The churches of the country would reflect the approaches that were prevalent in society. There have been several approaches that have attempted to relate to the steady stream of immigrants that have come to the United States.

One method was the "melting pot" approach. Peter Wagner, professor at Fuller Seminary, calls this the *assimilationist model.* Assimilation tried to eliminate any thing that was biracial, bicultural and bilingual.[2] Although the primary ingredient in the melting pot was English, the result was to be a new people based on the merger of many. If this emphasis was to be successful, each person in the mix had to give up his racial, lingual and cultural identity and become American.

Another approach was the *'anglo conformity'* model. It had many of the same characteristics as the assimilationist model. The end result was that everyone was to act and worship like a "White Anglo-Saxon Protestant." When I was in seminary, I spoke at the fall harvest festival in a New Hampshire church where I was a student pastor. The main course of the dinner was a special traditional dish called "Red-Flannel Hash." When the dinner was nearly over, my wife and I asked the people next to us when the Red-Flannel Hash was going to be served. They told us we had already eaten it. We thought we had eaten beets, but the people next to us said that Red-Flannel Hash consisted of the ingredients of a New England Boiled Dinner, ground up together. It looked like beets because beets made the dominant color. Frankly, I felt that there was something missing. The Red-Flannel Hash had all the ingredients, but didn't do justice to any one of them. Likewise, you can't make White Anglo-Saxon Protestants out of everyone.

Segregation was another approach used in dealing with the influx of immigrants into this country. This dealt with those people who couldn't be melted or couldn't be ground into hash. People who couldn't or wouldn't be assimilated were usually of dark skin, especially those with strong ties to their homeland. They were people who refused to give up their language, people who wanted to keep their culture. Many churches and other organizations covertly or overtly excluded these people from participation. They were excluded from worship and fellowship in churches because of prejudice.

Several years ago, Temple Baptist Church in Portland, Oregon, took part in the "I Found It" campaign. We were given the names of people from our area who indicated they wanted to receive free literature. Just north of the church there is a large community which is predominately inhabited by black people. Most of the people we went to visit were black. One of the ladies from our church asked if we should invite them to our church or recommend that they attend a black church in their own neighborhood. My immediate response was, "Invite them to come to Temple." After I told her that, I began to question whether or not that was the right answer to her question.

Temple Baptist Church is over 100 years old. It was formerly a Swedish Baptist Church. On an average Sunday morning there are rarely more than a dozen black people out of a total attendance of 500. Why would black people want to attend a service which was so culturally different? Our services were punctual, very short and very unemotional. Although the service is not liturgical, it is certainly viewed as being quite structured.

In the early '70s we brought many black children into our Sunday school by busing them in from other areas of the city.

Few of their parents came more than once or twice, for a special occasion. When the children began attending high school, only a few of the children who came on the buses stayed. We found that we could add numbers and different kinds of people by busing them in, but that practice did not increase fellowship or the process of assimilation.

In his book *The Kingdom Beyond Costs*, Liston Pope states that "eleven o'clock on Sunday morning is the most segregated hour in the week." He refers to the church as "the most segregated major institution in American society."[3]

Not only is the racial question whether blacks and whites should worship and fellowship together, but whether there should be any mixture of races. Our church adopted several Vietnamese families. They were hard workers and learned rapidly, but they were not comfortable in our congregation because of language and cultural barriers. Most of our people accepted them into our fellowship. There were some, however, who were not pleased with our spending time, energy and money on these new immigrants when so many people in our community were in need. One lady telephoned the church office. She was irate over our encouraging these displaced people to become part of our church. "Why are we helping all these 'Vietnamese people' when we have so many who need help right here?"

The tension between a homogeneous and heterogeneous congregation is one that every church faces. Although it is partially a racial issue, it cuts much deeper than that.

Physical and Emotional Diversity

Most of our churches and church services are designed to facilitate the worship and fellowship of people who do not have physical and emotional handicaps. Temple Baptist Church was built in 1927 and resembles a temple in its exterior appearance. It was well built and is well maintained. It was built to last, but it was not built to accommodate people with physical handicaps.

In order to enter the sanctuary there are many steps to climb. Neither the doorways nor the rest rooms allow people in wheelchairs to enter. The elderly and people who have problems with climbing would not feel very welcome. The architecture of many churches excludes not only the physically handicapped, but people whose eyes are sensitive to glare caused by modern lighting systems. Also, there are people who have various phobias, such as agoraphobia. These people are unable to function in large groups of people.

Mentally handicapped men who live in our neighborhood began attending worship services. They were different in appearance and mannerisms, and occasionally disruptive. Should we suggest that people who are different go some place else? Should we provide for people with all kinds of handicaps? Although no church has the facilities or capability to handle every kind of diversity, churches can learn to accommodate and assimilate a variety of people.

It is important for those of us who are not impaired to become aware of the needs that handicapped people have. Volunteers in the church could be assigned to assist individuals and sit with them during the service if help is needed and desired.

One Saturday we had a "Handicap Awareness" day. This was open to all church members. During the sessions each person experienced what it was like to be impaired in his sight or hearing. Also, people had to spend time in a wheelchair, etc. After awareness, the process of assimilation can begin. Churches need handicapped people as much as the handicapped need churches.

Educational Diversity

In the small rural church in Michigan where I was the pastor, I taught an adult Sunday school class. Instead of me reading the Scripture, one Sunday we went around the circle and asked each one read one verse. The next Sunday two of the couples didn't come back. Later I discovered the reason. The two husbands couldn't read. Although this may seem uncommon in the United States, there are many people who have educational limitations that debilitate their ability to function in the vast majority of churches.

There are probably people in your church who can help those who have not had educational opportunities — either through the church or through community services. Teachers might offer tutoring or, if qualified, teach English as a second language.

Many people who come to church have little or no knowledge of the Bible and biblical doctrines. Adult Sunday school teachers or small group study leaders can teach classes which provide basic scriptural information. Little things such as referring to page numbers in Scripture rather than asking people to turn to Obadiah will make it easier for those who are biblically illiterate to participate without fumbling through the pages. Do whatever you can to help people learn, so they don't feel left out because of their lack of knowledge.

Cultural Diversity

There are all kinds of people, especially in the city, who do not fit the traditional mold. Rather than strive for conformity, we need to celebrate diversity. No matter what our cultural backgrounds are, we can be enriched by differing cultures.

One way that has been effective in our church is to plan an "International Dinner." Individuals or Sunday school classes prepare foods that represent particular cultures. We allow expressions of various customs, art and music — not only in social gatherings, but as part of our worship experience.

Another type of cultural diversity comes from people who are products of the "counterculture." People whose appearance, attitude and actions are disruptive are not welcome in most churches. What should the church's attitude be toward these people? Some so-called "Jesus Freaks" do not feel comfortable in most churches, even though they are Christians. Others are considered radicals because of their social and political views. It certainly would be more comfortable without all this diversity, but it is not the purpose of the church to feel comfortable.

Family Diversity

Many groups describe their fellowship as being a "family church." Churches often tend to have a very limited perspective of the traditional family. The traditional model of the American family, where the father goes to work and mother stays home and raises children, is a minority. According to the 1980 Census Bureau statistics of 62 million American families, only 15% fit the old-fashioned stereotype. In almost 22% of the nation's families both parents are wage earners. In 11% there is only one parent. The remaining families have no children.

One pastor recently commented that they had no divorced people in his church. If a church has no divorced people among its constituency, something is drastically wrong. Divorced people are everywhere. The repercussions of divorce have affected all segments of society. Do childless couples, single parents, widows, divorcees, divorced-and-remarried people, unwed mothers, and those who have never been married feel welcome in our churches? Are the activities and ministries geared to meet their needs?

A person's family status should not be the basis of his or her acceptance. Members of extended and blended families need to support members of traditional families. Two-parent families can include single parents and their children in their family outings or even on vacations. Every adult is a role model to children. This is especially true of men. When the church body accepts and supports members of broken families, it reflects the love of Christ.

"Pluralism" — As Old as the Bible

The problem of distinguishing between "our kind" and "their kind" is not a new problem. It has existed throughout history, especially in the pluralistic society from which Christianity emerged. People's oneness in Christ, no matter what their racial, cultural, geographic, economic and educational status, is central to the gospel message. In Galatians 3:28 Paul states, "There is neither Jew nor Greek, slave nor free, male nor female, for you are all one in Christ Jesus." The same message is conveyed in other passages, such as in Colossians 3:11. "Here there is no Greek or Jew, circumcised or uncircumcised, barbarian, Scythian, slave or free, but Christ is all, and is in all." Through the years each generation in each geographical area has struggled with how to implement this oneness in a local congregation.

The tension between homogeneity and heterogeneity in society will not go away. Attempts to deal with it by means of assimilation or segregation have for the most part proved to be unacceptable. The church can be a leader in adjusting this tension. I believe that your church has a great opportunity to be an example, because of the uniqueness of the gospel.

Pluralism in our society is growing rapidly. Tetsunao Yamamori, a specialist in church growth, comments, "almost half the entire population of America today consider themselves ethnics. Church leaders at various levels are rightly voicing their concern about the ways and means of reaching America's ethnic minorities, as more and more churches 'caught' in racial and ethnic community changes are being forced to explore their future alternatives. Even churches in stable ethnic situations that desire to increase their outreach effectiveness to a minority population in their area are often at a loss as to how to reach these groupings of people."[4]

Adjusting the Tension

Any attempt to adjust the tension will be futile unless it deals squarely with the subject of prejudice. Prejudice is not merely a black-white issue, or even a racial issue. All of us have pride in our own country, our own family, our own church and our own friends. This pride, however, must never be the result of discrimination. Prejudice basically means prejudging one group of people to be superior or better than another group. But all mankind has been created in God's image. Any attempt in the church to promote or encourage homogeneity based on discrimination is wrong. We must search our hearts and confront our own prejudices before we can adjust the tension between acceptance and rejection of people who are not like us.

We need to learn acceptance of a Christian view of pluralism — a creative acceptance of the cultural diversity in our society. Previous approaches such as "assimilation" and "anglo-conformity" have not worked. Neither has segregation.

I believe that the best metaphor to describe a Christian view of pluralism is what Andrew Greeley describes as a "stew pot." In a stew pot, "each ingredient adds its flavor to every other ingredient, but all maintain their own identities and integrity. The final result is more than the sum of the parts. It is a new product, colorful and flavorful to a degree that would have been impossible for any of the ingredients taken alone."[5] Not only is our oneness emphasized, but our differences as well. In this approach no one loses his or her identity or respect, but each group and person has a contribution to make.

Both within a local church and within a local community, we can celebrate the different heritages and cultures of various groups. Congregations can exchange choirs and have a "pulpit exchange" with other congregations which are different from theirs. This brings an appreciation for the diversity and validity of other types of worship, music and preaching.

There may be groups within the community that have no facilities in which to meet. Many people have come to our communities from non-English speaking countries who need a place to worship, but do not have the necessary resources to afford a place of their own. Your church can offer the use of its facilities to one or more of these groups. If there are no diverse groups in your church's neighborhood, your church can help support efforts within your denominational fellowship to help groups who have needs. Your Home Missions Board has a wealth of information on multi-cultural fellowships, non-traditional and ethnic churches.

Look at Your Community

After your church examines its attitude, it must examine its community. All churches represent at least two communities — one where the people of the church live and work, and the other where the church is located. A church that doesn't minister to the community in which it is located needs to evaluate why it is located where it is. No church can isolate itself from the people which are part of its community.

Identify the kinds and groups of people that live in your community. These people become "target groups," people toward whom you target your outreach efforts. Make contact with them and find out what their needs are. Then look for ways to meet their needs. It is not enough to encourage a few individuals from these groups to attend your church. This is self-serving and a type of tokenism. Whether they attend the church or not, they need to feel welcome to do so.

One frustration that many churches experience is the feeling that they must attempt to meet the needs of every group in the community. This is neither possible nor practical. Cooperate with other churches in your community so that you don't duplicate efforts. If one church has a ministry to the hearing impaired, other churches don't need to do the same thing. If another church has a ministry to alcoholics, it is not necessary for your church to have the same ministry.

Every church needs to have a desire and an openness to ministry. Frank Tillapaugh in his book *Unleashing The Church* has developed an important concept in the Bear Valley Baptist Church in Denver, Colorado. It is called "relaxed concern."[6] After a church identifies the target groups in a community, it needs to proceed with confidence and with caution. Until the Holy Spirit leads people in the congregation to develop specific ministries to these people, the church should wait until this develops. Many churches have announced programs and then found that their efforts have died because no one felt burdened to follow through.

When your church discovers the racial or cultural diversity in your community, seek ways to recognize these groups and people. Attempting to bring in heterogeneous groups from other communities, whether from a sense of guilt or to achieve some type of racial or cultural balance, will not help either your church or those whom you bring in. But your church should reflect the community where it is located.

Homogeneity will be the pattern of most churches, but it must never be used to exclude individuals or groups, either passively or actively, from either membership or fellowship. A local church must be governed by the principles of love, not the principles of pragmatism. How your church proceeds will differ according to the community where it is located. Heterogeneity results from a desire to minister, never from a sense of false guilt.

All local churches need to ask themselves some very tough questions. Does the ministry of your church reflect the diversity in your community? Why does your church attract certain kinds of people? Does your church accept all kinds of people? Is your fellowship based on a spiritual unity or on outward conformity? Are the differences between "our kind" of people and "other kinds" of people natural or manufactured?

Let us celebrate both the sameness and the differences, without losing the one at the expense of the other.

Footnotes

1. Schaller, Lyle E., *The Parish Paper* Volume VI, No. IX, March 1977, (Richmond, IN).

2. Wagner, C. Peter, *Our Kind of People* (Atlanta: John Knox Press, 1979), p. 45.

3. *Ibid.*, p. 25.

4. Arn, Win, Editor, *The Pastor's Church Growth Handbook* (Pasadena: Church Growth Press, 1979), p. 171.

5. Wagner, C. Peter, *Our Kind of People*, p. 51.

6. Tillapaugh, Frank R., *Unleashing the Church* (Ventura, CA: Regal Books, 1982), p. 51, 52.

3

Who Is Supporting Whom?

The Tension Between the Church and Para-Church

My first confrontation with a para-church group took place in the middle 1960s. Two younger pastors whom I had met for the first time cornered me and started telling me about a new approach to evangelism called "The Four Spiritual Laws." Not only were they excited about this new method, but they proceeded to tell me that the traditional method that I had been using for years was outdated.

The more insistent they were, the more irritated I became. Up until this time para-church groups appeared to me to be primarily interested in supporting and extending the local church. For the first time I saw them in a different role. They were challenging the local church.

As these two young pastors continued to press their point, my irritation grew. The method of evangelism that I was using was tried and true. I had been taught how to witness to others about Jesus Christ at my local church, at the college I attended and at seminary. They all used the same method. The first step in witnessing to someone was to convince him that he was a sinner and was going to hell. If he agreed with that conclusion, then you told him about Jesus Christ and His plan of salvation. Finally you asked him to make a personal decision to receive Jesus Christ as Savior and Lord. These two pastors told me it was wrong to start with the fact that man was a sinner. The right place to start any presentation was with God and His love for men and women.

In the end, they persuaded me to at least try this new method. To my utter amazement, the first three people with whom I shared this booklet prayed to receive Christ. I wish I could say that the response ratio continued to be that good. One result of my confrontation with those two pastors, however, was that I began to see the value of new ideas, programs and methods which people were creating outside of the local church.

The tension that I felt when someone challenged the local church was very deep-seated. My commitment to the church was based on my doctrinal beliefs. Now there were people saying that the church had lost its effectiveness and needed to be replaced. This tension continued to grow.

Dr. John R. W. Stott says this is the age-old tension between *authority* and *freedom*. It is a sociological problem. Stott comments, "The term 'sodality' has been in use for several centuries, particularly in the Roman Catholic church, to describe 'a religious guild or brotherhood established for purposes of devotion or mutual help or action.' It is, therefore, a voluntary and usually rather loose association, which exists for a precise and limited purpose. In contrast 'modality' tends to be a more formal social structure with clearly defined membership and leadership, and with accepted rules for both . . . a local church is a 'modality,' while a para-church organization is a 'sodality.'"[1]

Para-church groups have existed for many years, but they were few in number until the 1960s. They were very specialized and most had limited geographical impact. "In the 10-year period from 1900-1919, 55 new agencies were begun; 1920-1939: 95; 1940-1959: 215; 1960-1979: 235."[2] What appeared to be a small, isolated phenomenon about 20 years ago has now gained such power and momentum in religious circles that some see it as a gigantic army which threatens to destroy the foundations of the local church.

By the middle of the 1980s the number of para-church groups had literally exploded. Jerry White in his excellent book, *The Church and The Para-Church*, observes that "The church in the second half of the twentieth century bears little resemblance to that of the first half and one of the dimensions is what I will term the 'para-local church' movement. The proliferation of organizations outside the traditional boundaries of the local church is so great as to stagger the imagination. Its potential input can either divide or build the kingdom of God."[3]

You Name It, They Do It

It is difficult to count all the groups that seemingly have challenged and invaded the territory which once belonged exclusively to the local church. Whether or not the church likes being invaded by outsiders, the para-church movement will not go away. Some of the categories of their service are: agriculture, aviation, camping, church planting, discipleship, education, evangelism, fund-raising, literature, management consultants, medicine, orphanages, radio, relief, television and translation.

Why has there been such a proliferation of organizations in the last half of the twentieth century? There are several reasons.

1. *Revival of Religious Interest.* In the early 1950s there were several revivals on the campuses of Christian colleges. Many men and women returned to college following time in the military service during World War II. They had a different

perspective of the world and a new religious fervor as well. Many churches were unwilling or unable to participate in the new wave of enthusiasm. New mission agencies came into being to facilitate sending those who were equipped to go.

2. *Belief That the Local Church Had Failed.* One founder of a para-church organization proclaimed that the church had been a colossal failure.[4] In fact, there was a tendency on the part of many to blame the church for all kinds of failures. One Christian disc jockey said that "Watergate would not have happened if the church had prayed for the President." The church became the scapegoat for many of the ills of the world.

3. *Anti-Institutionalism.* There was a worldwide revolt against institutional authority. Some of the countercultures were proclaiming "Jesus, yes; the church, no." People perceived a dichotomy between the church and its founder. Many in the church recognized the need for change, but the church was perceived as being so "...married to the 'status quo' that it either would not or could not change. The church, instead of being an agent of change, was seen as a buffer against it."[5]

4. *Irrelevancy of the Church.* Some were questioning if the local church had lost its purpose and meaning. One of the most scathing criticisms was that the church was more concerned with the physical structure than it was with the needs of people. The terms "edifice complex" and "fortress mentality" were used to describe this condition.

5. *Individualism.* America always has encouraged a pioneer spirit. There were many new ideas and creative approaches that the church was not equipped to handle. Those who wanted the freedom to experiment found little sympathy or support within the context of local churches.

6. *The Need For Specialization.* In order to take advantage of the tremendous opportunities caused by mobility and new methods of communication, Christianity had to develop specialists. The nature of the local church makes it more suitable

to meet general needs rather than those that require specialized skills and focus.

Although many local church leaders agreed that most churches needed renewal, they did not agree with the assessment that the local church was either dead or dying. Instead of welcoming para-church organizations as an "arm of the church," these leaders began to feel that the para-church had become the "hands of the church." Sometimes the hands were asking the local churches for money and other times the hands were around the churches' necks trying to choke them. For many people and churches it seemed to be a question of survival, and the para-church became the enemy.

Many of the more aggressive evangelistic groups were accused of "catching fish but expecting the local church to clean them." Their specialization often resulted in a lack of cooperation with local churches and other para-church groups. An unhealthy competitiveness arose on mission fields and on campuses. The outreach efforts, curriculum materials and relief work of various agencies were pitted against each other.

7. *Personality Clashes.* Most organizations (local church or para-local church) begin with a vision or with the dreams of one individual. The particular organization in which this person serves is not able or willing to permit its structure enough flexibility to accommodate this person's new ideas. Sometimes the individual leaves with the blessing of the parent organization and leadership. Other times he starts a new organization, not because of a clash of philosophies, but a clash of personalities. Many organizations are doing basically identical work, but the personalities of the leaders have kept them from working together. Even Paul and Barnabas went their separate ways when they could not agree over John Mark's usefulness. Rather than harming the effectiveness of their ministries, the division appeared to strengthen their endeavors.

8. *Unused Resource of Laity and Women.* During the last

two decades, pastors and other leaders encouraged people to discover their gifts and to use them. But two obstacles were constantly in the paths of laity in general and women in particular. One was the educational requirement. Many churches adopted the belief that a number of church responsibilities require a seminary degree. Not everyone wanted or could afford seminary training. Also, the structures of local churches could not accommodate the number and variety of ministries represented by laymen and women. People were seeking places where they could make a contribution and para-church groups were providing those places.

What Makes it *Para*-Church?

In order to avoid confusion with denominations and the universal church, Jerry White describes these out-of-the-church ministry groups as para-local churches. For brevity and clarity, I have adopted his definition. A "para-local church: any spiritual ministry whose organization is not under the control or authority of a local church." This definition puts the tension clearly in focus. The question we face is this: "How can there be freedom of groups and individuals to minister outside the local church and at the same time retain the authority of the local church?"

The following chart developed by Howard A. Snyder distinguishes between the biblical church and the para-church structures.[6]

The Biblical Church	Para-Church Structures
1. God's Creation	1. Man's Creation
2. Spiritual fact	2. Sociological fact
3. Cross-culturally valid	3. Culturally bound
4. Biblically understood and evaluated	4. Sociologically understood and evaluated

5. Validity determined by spiritual qualities and fidelity to Scriptures	5. Validity determined by function in relation to mission of the church
6. God's agent of evangelism and reconciliation	6. Man's agents for evangelism and service
7. Essential	7. Expendable
8. Eternal	8. Temporal and temporary
9. Divine revelation	9. Human tradition
10. Purpose to glorify God	10. Purpose to serve the church

This chart does not compare the local church and the para-church. It compares the church which was created by God and the para-church which was created by man. The descriptions do not make the para-church unnecessary, but put things in proper perspective. Every individual, whether a member of the local church or of the para-local church, or of both, should have as his or her purpose to glorify God.

Although the purpose and goals of a local and a para-church organization are similar, the groups function quite differently. Para-churches are designed to be specialists. Within the constituency of a local church there are usually young and old, the educated and the uneducated, the weak and the strong, the mature and the immature.

A philosophy that some para-church groups have is that leaders should "move with the movers." This means that you are to find people who are interested in growing and doing and spend your time with them. Leaders in the church are not able to do this. They need to spend time with the "movers," discipling and training people, but they also need time for "struggling with the stragglers." A shepherd cannot abandon those who are unproductive.

A local church often does not move very rapidly. In fact, to many people it seems to be standing still. Someone has said that the stanza of "Onward Christian Soldiers" that says "Like a mighty army moves the church of God, Brothers we are treading where the saints have trod," should be changed. A more accurate description might be, "Like a mighty tortoise moves the church of God, Brothers we are treading where we've always trod."

For those who have invested most of their ministry in a para-church organization, it is very difficult to reorient their thinking to accept the pace of the tortoise. A young man who had spent most of his ministry in a para-church organization became a deacon in our church. He was constantly critical of the fact that the church was not moving fast enough. He always referred to our church as "you"; he never could consider the church as "we."

A church, though it appears to move slowly, is theoretically self-sufficient. That is, it is designed to minister to itself. Because of the diversity within the church and the variety of spiritual gifts present, it is able to function like a body. It is not ministering to only one segment of the population, nor is it confined geographically. It should by nature always be universal in its scope.

What's At Stake

At a recent deacon's retreat we were going to discuss the book *Unleashing The Church* by Frank Tillapaugh. I asked each deacon to read the book before the retreat so we could discuss its implications for our church. In one section Tillapaugh discusses the validity of para-church ministries. He comments, "In the church we have developed a fortress mentality which says, 'We'll minister to anyone who will come and fit in with us.' The para-church has developed an unleashed mentality which says, 'We'll design ministries to go after those who won't come to us! Therefore, our models for target-grouping come mainly from the para-church ministries."[7]

A few days before the retreat, one of the deacons called me up and asked if he could take about ten minutes at the retreat to respond to the book. The deacon was a man who was very committed to the local church. He had served in World War II with General Patton in North Africa and recently had retired from a government job.

It was obvious when he started reading his paper on the relationship of the church to the para-church that he was very emotionally involved in the conflict. At one point in the paper he made a strong appeal to the rest of us that we should be on guard against the "paratroops" that were coming to destroy the church!

Tensions between the local church and the para-church have taken time to evolve. They were not immediately discernible when the first para-church groups emerged. Churches were the generalists and para-churches were the specialists. That seemed all right. Each was doing its own thing and the conflicts between organizations was minimal. Before long, however, tensions began to surface. Jerry White, who is both a para-church executive and a churchman, has identified four primary tensions between the church and para-church.[8]

Tension of Legitimacy. Nobody questions that Christ instituted the church. But was the church He had in mind the universal invisible church or the local visible church, or both? When Jesus said in Matthew 16:18, "I will build my church," did He include the para-church in that statement? Are para-church groups to work alongside the church or are they to be a replacement? Are there any functions or ordinances that are exclusive to the local church? The tension arises when you and others in your church try to answer these questions.

One Sunday evening we had a speaker from one of the large para-church evangelistic groups. He told us how, earlier in the day, he had baptized a lady in a nearby lake. Administering the ordinances (baptism and communion) as a representative of a para-church group did not present a problem to him. I regard baptism and communion as functions of the local church.

Tension of Authority. This tension has a broader scope than the previous one. Para-church organizations may or may not be biblically legitimate. An even deeper question that we grapple with is to whom are they accountable? Are they accountable to themselves, to other para-church groups, to the local church or to no one?

This results in a tension between the organizations over authority, and a tension between the individuals who minister in these organizations and people who minister in local churches.

One night while visiting some young people who were involved in a para-church ministry in Portland, I asked one of the leaders about the relationship of his ministry to the local church. He said that they were meeting together as staff of the organization and that was sufficient. When I asked him if any of the staff members of his local group were members of any church in Portland, he said that it wasn't necessary.

Tension of Leadership. In any organization the number of qualified leaders is always at a premium. Because of the time demands of both the church and para-church it is very difficult for leaders to function effectively in both simultaneously. On the one hand, the para-church has provided leadership opportunities not available in the local church. On the other, there has been a "leadership drain" from the local church to the para-church.

While I was serving a church in Michigan, one of the local campus ministries organized a musical group, largely composed of young people from the area churches. Many of these young people were the most talented and most active youth in their churches. They sang as a group in various places on Sunday evenings. Since most church youth groups at that time also met on Sunday evening, you can imagine the resentment of youth groups whose leaders were away singing during youth meeting times.

There is another subtle leadership tension that local churches experience. When people formerly employed in para-church leadership become leaders in a local church there is a question of allegiance. Many young people who went into para-church groups were motivated by their belief that the local church was not doing its job. Church consultant Lyle Schaller says that there are many people who now want to be leaders in the local church but who have never been to church. What he means by that statement is that people are coming from para-church organizations into local churches with very little exposure or experience in an ecclesiastical setting.

Tension of Finances. Everyone is after the same dollar. Essentially both the local church and the para-church are dependent on the resources provided by Christians. Local churches usually are restricted to the resources of their own people. Para-church groups freely seek funds from many sources.

Para-church groups contact local churches like yours for special funds. Or they can solicit support corporately from your church's mission budget. Then, through direct mail and direct contact with individuals, they contact members of your church for personalized support. As someone has said, para-church groups can "go in the front door through corporate giving or in the back door through individual donors." Local churches must rely upon individual giving.

Before our church offices were remodeled, we needed money to do the work. We had heavy financial commitments, especially to our Faith Promise approach to missions. Our leaders were reticent to make direct personal appeals to our members. That same week one of the members of the church informed me that a representative of a para-church organization in Southern California visited her and asked her to contribute money toward their organization's new offices.

Other areas of tension between the local church and the para-church include such issues as duplication of ministry, permanency, effectiveness, coordination and doctrinal differences.

Adjusting the Tension

The tension between the local church and the para-church is a complex one. If it is to be handled creatively, both groups will have to desire to work together. There are unifying principles that can bring the two groups together. Let me suggest several that will help us to be effective tension adjusters.

1. *Headship of Jesus Christ.* Jesus Christ ordained the church. He created it. There are many metaphors that are used to describe the church, such as building, bride, army, school, family and body. The description of the church as a body is probably the most basic. Jesus Christ is the Head. In Colossians 2:19 we read that it is from the Head that " . . . the whole body, supported and held together by its ligaments and sinews, grows as God causes it to grow." Jesus Christ and His Word are the final source and authority for any organization that considers itself Christian.

Organizations will change when the human leadership changes if they are not under the authority of the Lord Jesus Christ. Quite often Christian organizations are founded, built and controlled by a charismatic individual. People begin to rely upon him or her rather than the Lord. Although God has appointed human leaders, I can never use them as an excuse for unethical, immoral or illegal practices. All believers are ultimately under the authority of the Head, and responsible to Him first.

2. *Submission to the Authority of the Local Church.* Each member of the body needs to be personally accountable to the

local church. It is difficult to imagine how anybody can be submissive to the universal invisible church. Dr. Warren Wiersbe, former pastor of Moody Memorial Church, tells about a conversation that a friend of his had with a missionary. "'What group are you associated with?' my friend asked. The man replied, 'I belong to the Invisible Church.' My friend then asked, 'Well, what church are you a member of?' Again he got the answer, 'I belong to the invisible Church!' Getting a bit suspicious, my friend asked, 'When does this Invisible Church meet? Who pastors it?' The missionary then became incensed and said, 'Well, your church here isn't the true church. I belong to the Invisible Church!' My friend replied, 'Well, here's some invisible money to help you minister to the Invisible Church!' Now, my pastor friend was not denying the existence of the One Body. Rather, he was affirming the fact that the invisible Church (not a biblical term, but I will use it) ministers through the visible Church."[9]

Although we recognize that individuals must be accountable to the local church, para-church organizations usually cannot be and should not be accountable to the local church. Very few churches have the time or expertise to be involved in overseeing a para-church ministry.

Since it is impossible to be accountable to something that is invisible, we must be accountable to a visible church. No matter what responsibilities I have in a secular or para-church organization, I need to use my gifts, time and finances to strengthen my local church. Because the church functions as a body, all members are to submit to the leadership and direction of the church, as it is obedient to the will of God.

3. *Ministries Must Build Up the Body.* All ministries should strengthen the ministry of the local church. Para-church groups are to be the arms of the local church to help it accomplish its task of discipling all nations. Unfortunately, some people view the para-church as equal in importance with the local

church, and others see it as a replacement for the local church. These attitudes do not build up the visible Body of Christ.

The fruit of any organization's ministry should be channeled into the local church. It is imperative that the local church work with other organizations to improve ways of assimilating new people into its life and ministry.

4. *Methods Must Be Consistent With Scripture.* All methods within the church and the para-church should be governed by biblical principles. Any ministry group should also demonstrate financial accountability. Many para-church organizations have taken the first step, subscribing to some standards of responsible stewardship. Local churches also need to be financially accountable. The following are the standards adopted by the Evangelical Council For Financial Accountability:

1. Every member organization shall subscribe to a written statement of faith clearly affirming its commitment to the evangelical Christian faith.

2. Every member organization shall be governed by a responsible board, the majority of whose members shall not be employees/staff, and/or related by blood or marriage to such, which shall meet at least semiannually to establish policy and review its accomplishments.

3. Every member organization shall obtain an annual audit performed by an independent public accounting firm in accordance with generally accepted auditing standards with financial statements prepared in accordance with generally accepted accounting principles.

4. Every member organization shall have a functioning audit review committee appointed by the board, a majority of whom shall not be employees/staff and/or related by blood or marriage, for the purpose of reviewing the annual audit and reporting its findings to the board.

5. Every member organization shall provide a copy of its

current audited financial statements upon written request.

6. Every member organization should conduct its activities with the highest standards of integrity and avoid conflicts of interest.

7. Every member organization shall ensure that its fundraising appeals clearly identify the purposes and programs to which the donations will be applied and shall ensure that these donations are used for the purpose for which they were raised.

Your church, in its relationships with para-church groups, should insist on these financial standards.

5. *Biblical Basis for Purpose and Belief.* The purpose of each organization should be clearly stated. Doctrinal beliefs should be listed and subscribed to by members of the organization. The doctrinal distinctives are stated quite clearly by local churches, but because of the wide basis of financial support found in para-church groups, sometimes the doctrinal statements are not published, or when they are, they are ambiguous. Know what you're supporting.

6. *Policies of Support Must Be Understood.* The most important document in the local church where I was a pastor is the mission policy. I do not know how a church can function without one. There are many important questions that your mission policy can clearly answer. Who is your church going to support? How many people are you going to support? How much money are you going to give?

Temple Baptist Church in Portland, Oregon is a member of the Baptist General Conference. Many representatives of para-church groups belong to the church. We have established a priority for our giving. We direct our gifts in the following order of significance:

1. Our own members serving in Baptist General Conference ministries.

2. Other Baptist General Conference members serving in Baptist General Conference ministries.
3. Our own members engaged in evangelical ministries under an approved mission board or agency.
4. Agencies and individuals working within metropolitan Portland.
5. Other evangelical ministries represented by members of Temple Baptist Church.
6. Other approved missionary organizations and agencies.

7. *Recognition of Contributions of Para-Church Organizations.* Jerry White lists several areas where para-churches have provided training and direction for local churches. Some of the areas are as follows: Missions, mobilization of the laity, a place for women, evangelism, instruction and training in ministry skills, discipleship and personal growth, small group concept, education and innovation.[10]

Many churches exclusively use materials published by their denominations. A number of para-church groups have led the way in producing curriculum and other materials for local churches. Before deciding which material to use, teachers and leaders in churches should see what para-church groups offer. When material is selected, they need to publicly acknowledge the group that supplied it. But all materials must obviously first meet the needs of the church.

8. *Evaluation of Continuing Need for the Organization.* Very few organizations are allowed to die. Both local churches and para-churches should cease to exist when they no longer have a purpose for being. Not every organization that is started will be successful. It is important to admit failure and be willing to be expendable. Organizations are like taxes. New ones are added, but rarely are the existing ones ever dropped. Be on guard against the twin problems of irrelevancy and duplication.

It is very difficult to drop an organization from a church

budget. Once a para-church ministry begins to receive financial support, individuals in the church will continue to support its cause even though it may no longer be effective. Your church's mission committee should establish a yearly review to evaluate each group. This evaluation can determine whether or not to continue support for another year.

9. *Encouragement, Prayer and Financial Support*. When churches expect individuals to be accountable to their church, then they must support these individuals. It may not be possible to support all para-church employees that go to your church, but you can encourage them and pray for them on a consistent basis.

A member of our church who worked for a campus ministry wrote the following letter about her acceptance and support by the local church:

"I just wanted you to know how much I appreciate you and all of Temple. You really set the pace in reaching out to people in your friendly ways — *always* remembering names, etc. (amazing!). I'm praying and confident in how mightily the Lord will be using you. I am very proud of you and your godly, lived-out convictions. I appreciate you and Bob and Terry as you all so inclusively and lovingly care for and reach out through the many parts of the body. One big thing that drew me to Temple was how supportive and appreciative you all were of Campus Crusade for Christ. It is so refreshing to be around such positive and encouraging people. I know that same attitude is there towards other organizations as well. So thanks! Thanks for letting Jesus shine brightly through you and Temple as you give leadership. I am so grateful to be a part of our family there and be so loved and prayed for too!"

The para-church needs the local church. The local church needs the para-church. Although the local church can exist without para-church groups, it can not function well. A para-church can increase the effectiveness of a local church by adding arms. Before you support para-church ministries with your money, time and prayer, make sure the arms are attached to the body and under the control of the Head.

Footnotes

1. *Co-operating in World Evangelization: Lausanne Committee For World Evangelization*, Wheaton, IL, 1983, pp. 13-15.

2. "Do We Need the Organization?" *Christian Leadership Letter*, World Vision, Monrovia, CA, October 1983.

3. White, Jerry, *An Uneasy Marriage: The Church and the Parachurch* (Portland, OR: Multnomah Press, 1983), p. 7.

4. "The Great Evangelical Power Shift," *Eternity*, Philadelphia, PA, Evangelical Ministries, 1979, p. 18.

5. Hadden, Jeffrey K., *The Gathering Storm In the Churches* (Garden City, NY: Doubleday and Co., Inc., 1970), p. 251.

6. *Ibid., Co-operating In World Evangelization*, p. 95.

7. Tillapaugh, Frank R., *Unleashing the Church* (Ventura, CA: Regal Books, 1982), pp. 52,53.

8. *Ibid., An Uneasy Marriage*, pp. 30-33.

9. Wiersbe, Warren W., *Be Rich* (Fullerton, CA: Victor Books, 1976), p. 103.

10. *Ibid.* Jerry White, pp. 105-110.

4

Paid for Being Good

The Tension Between Pastoral Staff and the Members

"Where do you work?"

I had just completed four years of college, three years of seminary and a year of further study. After eight years of education I was now in my first full-time position. I answered the lady's question with a sense of satisfaction. "I am the pastor of the Robinson Baptist Church."

"Oh yes, I know that," she said, "but where do you work?"

At first I thought she was joking. But a few days later I learned that I was the first pastor in this little community to have his total source of income from a church. Every other pastor she had known had held a 40-hour-a-week job and did his pastoral work in addition to his regular job.

A few weeks later I was visiting in the home of one of the church families. A relative of the people I was visiting came to the house during my visit. When he found out I was a pastor, he asked, "Why are you here?" "I'm visiting," I replied. "Do you get paid for doing that?" "Yes, I do," I responded. "That's really something," he said in amazement, "I visit all the time and no one ever pays me a cent."

Twenty years later I and one of the elderly members of another church were discussing which person in the church should do a particular task. His suggestion was that someone on the church staff should do it. "You guys get *paid* for being good," he said with a twinkle in his eye. "The rest of us are good for *nothing.*"

Two Classes of People?

Whether people are serious about the matter or joke about it, the separation of church members into two distinct classes of people results in a tension in every local church. The two classes are usually identified as clergy and laity. Behind this classification are many issues that cause tension and conflict in the church. Some of these issues are: Vocation or avocation; part-time or full-time; temporary or permanent; professional or nonprofessional; trained or untrained; forefront or background; primary role or secondary role; volunteer or paid; and ordained or unordained.

The tension between clergy and laity is not simply one that is relegated to a particular part of the country, or a particular size of church, or a particular kind of church. It is an issue that centers around the way the body of believers should function. Many people have been led to believe that there are basically two parts to the body — those that do the work and those who support those who do the work. These two parts act differently, look differently and speak differently. Therefore they are to be treated differently.

A double standard still exists in the minds of many people. One pastor that I knew in the late 1960s was serving a congregation in New England. Although he had been the pastor there for over thirty years, he was earning a salary of less than

$5,000. The church treasurer was making more than twice that much at his secular job. One day I asked the treasurer if he would be willing to work for the salary that his pastor was making. "Sure I would, if I were a pastor!" he replied. He expected the pastor to be a living example of sacrifice and frugality in every area of life.

The idea that there are to be two separate classes of people exists in the minds of many of the people in the pews. It also thrives in the teaching of many pastors. It comes from a mis-understanding of the nature of the church. One of the basic concerns of the church is one of identity. The image of the church as God's people is a primary one. Historically, God has always had a chosen people. In Deuteronomy 7:7-9 we read: "The Lord did not set his affection on you and choose you because you were more numerous than other peoples, for you were the fewest of all peoples. But it was because the Lord loved you and kept the oath he swore to your forefathers.... Know therefore that the Lord your God *is* God; he is the faithful God, keeping his covenant of love to a thousand generations of those who love him and keep his commands."

All of God's people in New Testament times are pictured as being members of the universal invisible church. The New Testament writers use many metaphors to express both the reality and the function of the church. In the book of Ephesians the church is described as a temple for worship, a family for fellowship, a school for learning, a bride for affection and an army for battle. Perhaps the most descriptive metaphor, however, is the one found in Ephesians 1:22,23: "And God placed all things under his feet and appointed him to be head over everything for the church, which is his body, the fullness of him who fills everything in every way." The church is a body which is to be controlled by the Head, Jesus Christ.

Because there is only one Head there cannot be two classes of people. Every member of the body receives his energy and direction from the same person. Dr. Ray Stedman in his book *Body Life* comments, "The church is not a conglomeration of individuals who happen to agree upon certain ideas. It is bound together as an organism in a bodily unity. It is true that a body is an organization but it is much more than an organization. The essence of a body is that it consists of thousands of cells with one mutually shared life . . . a body is formed by the extension of one original cell which grows until it becomes a mature body in which every cell shares the original life. That is the secret of a body — all parts of it share life together. It is the sharing of life that makes a body different from an organization. An organization derives power from the association of individuals, but a body derives its power from the sharing of life."[1] The church is made up of people, each of whom is a cell in the body performing a vital function. No part is secondary or unimportant — neither pastor nor laymen.

The distinction then between clergy and laity is not a scriptural one. Jesus and the men whom He chose considered themselves to be servants. In 1 Peter 5:2,3, Peter exhorts the elders to "Be shepherds of God's flock that is under your care, serving as overseers — not because you must, but because you are willing, as God wants you to be; not greedy for money, but *eager to serve;* not lording it over those entrusted to you, but being examples to the flock." Although these men were given the responsibility to be shepherds of God's flock, they always considered themselves to be servants.

The distinction between clergy and laity did not come about overnight. It evolved over hundreds of years. Ecclesiastical traditions became a part of Western culture. The meaning of the word 'minister' probably changed in society when the church ceased to function like a body.

The early church met together, ate together, served together and were persecuted together. When the persecution waned and Christianity became more acceptable and respectable, the need for daily reciprocal ministry became less of a priority. With respectability the nature of ministry changed, and so did the definition of the word. The term ministry simply means serving. A minister is a servant. Originally, a minister was one who served others in love. Another word for servant is the word deacon. A deacon was one who waited on tables.

Since then, a different meaning of the word ministry has emerged. The broad, general sense of the term has given way to a more narrow technical definition. Staff members in a local church are now "ministers." Although the Bible defines ministry in the broader sense, our common cultural and ecclesiastical meaning is usually the narrow one.

The tensions between clergy and laity do not revolve around one issue. They can be seen through many ecclesiastical and geographical lenses. There are at least five issues that contribute to this tension within the body.

Issue of Qualification

The New Testament emphasizes that when an individual is adopted into the family of God, he or she is given a spiritual gift(s) that allows him to become a productive servant. A spiritual gift is not the same as a natural talent or ability. In a rural church where I served in Michigan, we had several teachers from the local school who also taught Sunday school classes. The best teacher in the Sunday school, however, was not any of those teachers, but the school custodian. He could not teach in the public school because he lacked the educational qualifications. But he taught in our Sunday school because he had the spiritual qualifications.

Spiritual gifts are given at the time of regeneration, but it may take time for us to discover and develop these gifts. We discover them as we experiment in areas of Christian ministry, evaluate the effectiveness in using the gift, and wait for other believers to evaluate our use of the gift. Because all Christians are gifted, there are no parts of the human body or of the spiritual body that are unimportant. Lay "ministers" are as necessary and as valuable as paid staff.

When I was serving in my first church, I remember using a sermon illustration which described a particular organ of the body. I said it had no function. After the sermon a lady very kindly explained how important that organ was. She told me she had been very ill because that organ was not functioning properly.

In 1 Corinthians 12:22-25 Paul explains, ". . . those parts of the body that seem to be weaker are indispensable. . . . God has combined the members of the body . . . so that there should be no division in the body, but that its parts should have equal concern for each other." The church body needs a variety of gifts in order to function properly. The distribution of gifts is unequal. At first glance this may seem unfair, but equality means sameness. And sameness eliminates everything that makes you a unique person. God in His sovereign grace has qualified each individual with the gift(s) that is essential for building up the entire body.

Issue of Positions

Just as God has given us different gifts, He also has placed us in different positions within the body. It is as important to understand our roles as it is to understand our gifts. Roles are positions established by God that place us in relationships. For instance, in families there are fathers, mothers and children. In a business there are employees and employers. Likewise, in a church God has established certain positions to help the body of believers to function properly.

In Ephesians 4:11,12 we read, "It was he who gave some to be apostles, some to be prophets, some to be evangelists, and some to be pastors and teachers, to prepare God's people for works of service, so that the body of Christ may be built up..." God has appointed and called some to be pastors and teachers.

One Sunday morning a man came into our worship service carrying a briefcase. (I always get uneasy when I see someone come into a church carrying a briefcase. I wonder what he wants to sell). After the service one of the ushers told me that the man was a minister, and was upset because he wasn't asked to sit on the platform. The next week a couple of us went to visit him. We asked him what church he was from. He said that he didn't have a church. "How did you become a minister?" I asked. "Someone told me that all I needed to do was to pray and ask God to make me a minister. I prayed and He made me a minister." Then he blurted out, "Now I want my own church, my own pulpit and my own set of keys."

It was obvious that he had confused the terms minister and pastor. All pastors are ministers, but not all ministers are pastors. Those whom God has called to be pastors are neither better nor more important than the people to whom they minister. Pastors and teachers have received gifts and skills not existing in the congregation, and the ability to mobilize other gifts and skills which are potentially in the congregation. Those who are called to certain positions in the church are not to displace the ministry of the people of God, but to mobilize it and supplement it.

Issue of Availability

Ever since I can remember, I was challenged to consider going into "full-time" Christian work. Full-time Christian work was synonymous with the positions of church staff member or missionary. These people spent all of their time in church-related or missionary-related activities. All other people were called to "part-time" Christian work. That meant that they spent most of their time earning a living in a secular job or at home when not involved with church-related work.

Elton Trueblood claimed that the distinction between "full-time" and "part-time" is not a biblical one. He said there should be only one kind of Christian — a "full-life" Christian. A believer is to view his or her entire life as a "living sacrifice to God." In Romans 12:1 Paul urges the church at Rome, ". . . in view of God's mercy, to offer yourselves as living sacrifices, holy and pleasing to God — which is your spiritual worship."

Part of the reason for the false distinction between "full-time" and "part-time" is another misunderstanding — that the term "church" is synonymous with what happens within the four walls of the building.

Dr. Grant Howard, professor at Western Conservative Baptist Seminary, explains that we should not make a distinction between the church *and* the world. Rather, we should think of the church as *in* the world. He illustrates this idea with the example of a football team. When the church meets for worship and instruction, it is like football players in the huddle. When you and others leave your church building you do not cease to be the church any more than the football team ceases to be players when they leave the huddle and goes to the scrimmage line. There are no substitutes and no spectators. It must be a total effort by the entire team. Somebody needs to be the coach, but to be most effective he should be a "player-coach."

We are all full-life Christians, serving God both in our church building and every moment we are outside of it.

Issue of Employment

If every Christian is a minister who has been gifted by God, then we can logically assume that every Christian should have a ministry. Doug Anderson of Nehemiah Ministries has said that after studying hundreds of churches he sees a 20-30-50 rule. It is a consistent pattern in churches all over the country. In giving, for example, he says that 20% of the people give 80% of the money, 30% of the people give 20% of the money, and 50% don't give anything. He says the same percentage holds true in regard to ministry in the church. 20% do 80% of the work, 30% do 20%, and 50% do nothing.

The unemployment rate in the church is much worse than in our country. And at the same time there are also people who are greatly overemployed. Using the analogy of a football game again, someone has said that there are 22 men on the field badly in need of rest and 100,000 spectators in the stands badly in need of exercise. Is your church like this?

Marshall Shelley in his book *Well-Intentioned Dragons* points to a dilemma that exists in many churches. "When Richard Halverson was pastor of First Presbyterian Church of Hollywood, California, a church of seven thousand members, he discovered to his amazement only 365 were required to fill the church slots — choirs, boards, committees, teaching posts, and that was assuming each person could hold only one position. This meant, of course, that the overwhelming majority of the church could never have a ministry within the institution."[2]

In most churches there simply are not enough ministries to go around. When people see that the church is functioning and the opportunities for ministry are filled, they file for unemployment. Many people see their responsibility in church as supporting and observing those who are doing the work. A lot of Spirit-given talent is going to waste.

Issue of Remuneration

For many years the pastor was the only person in church congregations who received any remuneration. If larger churches were to function effectively, however, many other people were needed to fill key positions. People were needed to build and maintain the building, play musical instruments and sing, teach Sunday school, work in the nursery, perform secretarial functions and pay the bills. All of these people and many more worked joyfully as volunteers without a thought of being paid. Some things weren't done very well and sometimes conflicts among the workers caused problems in the church, but the broad sense of involvement and ownership far outweighed the difficulties.

Things came to a head between paid and volunteer workers about a generation ago. It not only affected churches but many other volunteer associations such as hospitals, service organizations, community groups and fraternal clubs. Churches began hiring architects and building contractors to design and construct their buildings. The number of people willing to maintain the building after it was built began to decline. Few people were willing to sign up as church custodian or to cut the grass. Fewer people volunteered to direct the youth ministry, work in the nursery, or cook the church dinners.

According to church consultant Lyle Schaller, "The world from which volunteers are drawn has changed. More women are employed outside the home. Between 1960 and 1980, the number of men in the American labor force increased by fourteen million, but the number of women employed outside the home increased by twenty-two million. Furthermore, the number of persons with two or more jobs increased from 3.7 million in 1965 to 4.9 million in 1982. Between ten and twelve million people work nights, meaning they usually are not available for evening meetings or programs."[3]

Volunteers are not usually members of the church staff, do not work for long periods of time and are not paid. But they should be committed to excellence. No one who is serving the Lord should be excused for inferior workmanship.

Understanding the issues involved does not eliminate the tension between clergy and laity, but it provides a basis for making a healthy adjustment. Simply changing the nomenclature will not solve this complex issue. The issues of qualification, positions, availability, employment and remuneration should be examined before this tension can be positively adjusted.

Making Good Adjustments

The clergy/laity tensions can be adjusted to produce a proper balance among the members of the body. Here are some steps which will help you and each member of your church search for a productive place to minister.

1. *Redefine the Terms*

When I was a seminary student serving a small country church in New Hampshire, my wife and I spent a couple of days vacationing in the mountains near the church. We stopped at a grocery store to buy food for the weekend. The owner asked what kind of work I did. When I told him that I was a seminary student he responded, "We give a discount to members of the cloth." I had never heard that expression before. According to the dictionary the word "cloth" means "the professional dress of a clergyman." Through the years I have seen how terms like cloth, clergy and cleric have been detrimental to people's concept of ministry. The clergy are seen as ecclesiastical *officials.* Not too many officials are considered to be *servants*, but that is what the Bible calls them.

The definition for laity on the other hand is simply "all those outside the clergy." Dr. Joseph Aldrich, President of Multnomah School of the Bible, suggests that instead of using the terms "clergy" and "laity" we use the term "claity." Since clay often refers to that which is "human," claity helps me to realize that none of us walk on water, unless we know where the rocks are.

Each individual should define what he or she means by the term "minister." There are no second-class citizens or vestigial organs in the body. Redefining the terms will not in itself balance the tension, but each individual needs to know for himself, "What does being a minister mean to me?"

2. *Recover the Ministry*

The term minister is a good one. It describes the function of the people of God. But it confuses the roles of the people of God. In most people's minds both within and outside the church the term minister refers to those who are members of the clergy. Start referring to all members of the body as ministers.

A pastor friend of mine explained his view of ministry to the congregation in his first message as the new pastor of the church. "I am not the minister. You are not the ministerees. We are all ministers. We are all ministerees. . . I'm looking forward to growing together to the point where everyone in our congregation senses how we have been uniquely gifted of God. And as we grow together over the years, we will sense. . . a complete happiness and being at peace with ourselves because we realize that maybe for the first time in our lives we are fulfilling the function of ministry for which God has gifted us. Ministry is a reciprocal affair."

It may not be possible to redefine the term minister as it is used in our society today. If the church is to be what God intended it to be, however, we must recover the function of ministry. Ministry includes both clergy and laity. Orien Johnson in his book *Recovery of Ministry* comments about this process of recovering the biblical function of ministry. "We have seen obstacles in the traditional meanings of words and thought patterns. But science constantly contends with similar obstacles in the space race. Old concepts of gravity, speed, transportation and communication have given way to new and wider dimensions than we thought were possible. This development should encourage us to find deeper meanings to words we have traditionally used to convey our thoughts concerning ministry."[4]

After accepting the fact that each individual is a minister, he or she must ask him- or herself, "Am I available to be used in a ministry?" If you are ready, then report for duty. Not all areas of ministry are exciting, but all can be satisfying if done for the King.

3. Provide Opportunities for Ministry

Many people are not involved in ministry because professionals are already doing the work. That makes it difficult for these people to find a place in the system. It is especially difficult for new members, younger people and single people (usually women) to find a viable ministry within the existing structure.

If you cannot find a place to minister within the existing structure of your church, you may want to create a ministry outside the structure. Opportunities vary from community to community. Some examples are being an aid in a hospital or school, reading to the blind, providing meals or shopping for the elderly, tutoring handicapped or international students and assisting in day care centers.

Each person is part of a community. A natural place to start is with the people nearby. If you do not know anyone in your immediate neighborhood who needs your services, contact volunteer agencies. These are days of *ad hocism*. Don't wait for an invitation. If you knock on a few doors, it won't take long to find your place.

Learn to recognize ministry opportunities that exist within your sphere of influence. If you think you can develop a ministry to meet a specific need of a certain group of people, then check with your church leaders to see whether or not it can be incorporated within the current system, or if it should remain outside the system. If you are in a leadership position, recognize and verbally acknowledge the need people in your church have to minister. Look for ways to spur people on in their service.

4. *Enlist, Equip, and Evaluate Ministries*

Lyle Schaller states that, "Protestant congregations can be divided into two categories. The first and the smaller of the two in terms of number of churches might be described as the high-demand churches. These congregations expect a lot of each member. . . . By contrast, many more Protestant congregations fit into a second category that can be identified simply as 'voluntary churches.' These congregations display more of the characteristics of the voluntary association, in which each member retains the right of withdrawal, than of the closely knit and highly disciplined communities that are found among the high-demand churches."[5]

All churches need ministers for ministry. Churches that either voluntarily or involuntarily teach members that ministry is optional will have a much more difficult time getting people involved than those that expect people to serve. There are many ways to motivate people: by loyalty, by expectations, by rewards, by a sense of obligation, by guilt, by fear, by concern for others and by enabling them to become better Christians.[6] Your church's nominating committee or some other group or individual needs to recruit people to do the work of the church.

Most people will not volunteer. They need to know that there is a need. Don't ask for volunteers. Very few will respond and sometimes those who do will not be qualified or prepared. Quite often in a church, "The willing aren't able and the able aren't willing." Leaders in the church should challenge people individually, encouraging them to experiment in different ministry areas until they find one which fits their gifts, abilities and the time they have available.

Not only is enlisting people a continual task, but your church has an ongoing responsibility to train people for their ministries. Within your church, workshops for teacher training and leadership seminars can be provided. In urban areas local schools offer adult education courses. All kinds of training materials are available on video cassettes. And seminaries often provide extension centers with video tapes of a variety of biblical, theological and ministry courses.

Every ministry in your church needs periodic evaluation of the effectiveness of its ministers and its effectiveness. Too often we measure activity instead of results. It may be necessary to drop certain ministries and redeploy those who have lost their effectiveness. It is all right for your church to drop or change a ministry. But do it in a way that avoids making people feel guilty.

Our church at one time was involved in a large bus ministry. Many high school and college young people gave every Saturday and half a day Sunday to visiting homes and picking up children. The young people were expected to do this every week without a break. If they dropped out after a period of time, they were made to feel that they had "let the church and the Lord down." One day my daughter came to me frustrated. She sighed, "Daddy, the only way that I can get out of this bus ministry is go away to college."

Sometimes ministries are no longer needed. People have to find new things to do. Don't add guilt to the stress of making ministry changes.

5. *Pay All Ministers*
It is hard to use the New Testament to make a case for paying

or not paying church workers. Those who think workers should be self-supporting point to the passages where pastors, teachers and evangelists in the church supported themselves from their secular employment. The phrase, "tent-making" ministry came from Paul's occupation of making tents to support his ministry (see Acts 18:1-3, 20:34). In these and other passages Paul appears to describe his personal situation, rather than a set of commands that other workers should follow.

On the other hand, some who argue that people who labor in the church should be paid quote such verses as 1 Cor. 9:14, where Paul writes, "...the Lord has commanded that those who preach the gospel should receive their living from the gospel." Other Bible verses which seem to support this idea can be found in Gal. 6:6; Phil. 4:14-16; and 1 Tim. 5:17,18.

Many churches are hung up on the question of who should get paid and how much. Every minister in the church, whether employed or volunteer, must be *paid*. The question is not how much, but *what* their payment will be. Lyle Schaller in his book *The Pastor and People* states, "The compensation for volunteer service takes many forms. These include the feeling of satisfaction that often accompanies a positive response to a real need, a sense of personal fulfillment, satisfaction with a job well done, 'repayment' for services received from others, reinforcement of a sense of personal worth or value, a response to the obligations incurred by membership in an organization, 'brownie points,' a channel for expressing neighbor-centered love, prestige, status, public recognition, anticipation of rewards in heaven, 'evening the score,' fellowship and the opportunity for personal growth, development and learning."[7]

For many volunteers, payment in money for services rendered would neither increase their effectiveness nor affect their attitude toward their job. Workers in a church do have a right, however, to expect adequate working conditions, materials to work with and sufficient resources to do the job. And they have a right to receive proper training, consistent supervision and appreciation for the work they are doing, especially from the church staff.

Each person in a church is a minister and therefore has a responsibility to minister. God has called some to equip and encourage individuals to do the work of the ministry. These are often the paid staff. What is your ministry? Do you need to enlist others to work with you? Your church needs you. Your community needs you. You are important. If you are not involved and want to be, don't wait to be asked. Pray about it and try something.

Footnotes
1. Stedman, Ray C., *Body Life* (Regal Books: Glendale, CA, 1972) pp. 24,25.
2. Shelley, Marshall, *Well-Intentioned Dragons* (Waco, TX: Word), pp. 85,86.
3. *The Parish Paper*, November 1982, Vol. 12, Number 5, Lyle E. Schaller, Editor.
4. Johnson, Orien, *Recovery of Ministry* (Valley Forge, PA: Judson Press, 1972), p. 14.
5. Schaller, Lyle E., "The Christian Ministry": 'High Demand or Voluntary Church?' (Richmond, IN: The Christian Century Foundation, September 1984).
6. *Ibid.*
7. Schaller, Lyle E., *The Pastor and The People* (Nashville, TN: Abingdon, 1973), p. 81.

5

Who's In Charge?

The Tension Between Power and Authority

A new church in a Southern California suburb stopped growing. The leading layman of the church, who also happened
to be one of its founders found himself in continual conflict
with the pastor, who had come to the church after it had been
organized. Most of their conflicts centered around the question, "Who's in charge?" Finally, they reached an impasse. Someone described the situation as both looking "eyeball to eyeball
and neither of them being willing to blink."

During the first few years of the church's existence the layman
held most of the elected positions in the church. As the church
grew, developing an organizational structure which included
a constitution and bylaws, he no longer held elected posts.
However, he still held many other positions of influence. He
was the choir director, the song leader and the adult Sunday
school teacher. His influence resulted from the positions that
he held, from the fact that he was a professional man in the
community and because he made large contributions to the

church.

Quite often, in matters of church business, he would take the opposite side of an issue from the pastor. Increasingly, this layman found himself as a leader of the minority. When he didn't get his way, he would threaten to drop all of his responsibilities. On a few occasions he said he was going to leave the church. Because many people felt they would not be able to continue as a church without him, they always begged him to stay. Through his influence and power, he was able to run the church, even though he held no elected office and was in the minority. There was never any question about "who was in charge."

In a rural Midwest community, there were two families who held most of the positions in the local church. Of the six deacons, two were a father and son and three of the others were brothers. The oldest brother was the patriarch of his family. Neither of his brothers voted against him on a crucial issue. He was the leader in the church and in the community. No decisions were made without his approval. As long as he was careful not to offend the other large family in the church, his word was law. Later, when he no longer held the same elected positions, he still was the "church boss." No one in that church would have any difficulty answering the question, "Who's in charge?" As long as the pastor agreed with this man's position, everything went smoothly.

In an established ethnic urban church there were two men who had held leadership positions for several decades. Although neither of them had large families in the church, both had large followings. Each became the spokesperson for people with differing philosophies.

The two men were not enemies. Rather, they were considered "friendly antagonists." One of them represented the younger, more progressive people in the church. The other man represented those who held a more traditional view and wanted to preserve the status quo. Years after they ceased to hold any official capacity in the church, they still carried as much influence, maybe even more. It was nearly impossible to make any major decisions without one of these men's approval. Even after these two men died, they continued to have an impact on the direction that the church took.

"Who's in charge?" This crucial question is not confined to any geographical area or historical era. The New Testament church experienced many of the same struggles that churches have today. Sometimes the struggle is between two individuals, sometimes it is between two groups. In Acts 15 we see examples of both kinds. In Acts 15:1,2, we read, "Some men came down from Judea to Antioch and were teaching the brothers: 'Unless you are circumcised according to the custom taught by Moses you cannot be saved.' This brought Paul and Barnabas into *sharp dispute* and *debate* with them." Later on, in Acts 15:36-39 ". . . Paul said to Barnabas, 'Let us go back and visit the brothers in all the towns where we preached the word of the Lord and see how they are doing.' Barnabas wanted to take John, also called Mark, with them, but Paul did not think it wise to take him because he had deserted them in Pamphylia and had not continued with them in the work. They had such a *sharp disagreement* that they parted company. . ."

In retrospect it appears that Paul was correct in his first encounter with the Judaizers (the circumcision party). But in the second instance he appeared to be wrong in his dispute with Barnabas.

The question that people need to answer is not always who is right, but who is in charge. All of us know that although the majority usually rules, the majority is not always right. Back in my early years of ministry I was a substitute teacher. One day I was teaching in a one-room school house. It was time for the three fifth graders to come to my desk for their math lesson. I didn't have an answer book so I asked the children,

"How will I know which answer is right?" One of the children quickly responded, "Any time two of us have the same answer, it's right." The majority isn't necessarily right (even if they are unanimous) in the one-room school house or the church.

Power and Authority

The question of "Who is in charge?" in the church is such a basic one that every local congregation needs to understand what it implies. The basic tension is not one between right and wrong, but between power and authority. Every type of church structure experiences the same tension. Before we can adequately deal with the question of "Who's in charge?", we need to understand the place that power and authority have in the decision making process.

Authority, according to the dictionary, is "the *right* a person or group has to govern, control, or command." Authority can be viewed from a psychological, sociological, or an ecclesiastical perspective. For instance, Anthony Campolo in his book *The Power Delusion* defines authority from a sociological perspective "as the ability to get others to want to do your will because they recognize that what you ask is legitimate and right."[1]

Power, on the other hand, according to the dictionary refers to the *ability* to act or do. Campolo defines power as "the prerogative to determine what happens and the coercive force to make others yield to your wishes — even against their own will."[2] In our culture power implies manipulation, abuse or force. This meaning is seen in such terms as nuclear power, black power and political power.

In the Scripture, however, the terms authority and power are both positive terms, when they are given by God. In John 1:12, ". . . to all who received him, to those who believed in his name, he gave the right to become children of God." Jesus gave us the authority to be the children of God. In Acts 1:8 we see that the Holy Spirit gave us the power to witness. "...you will receive power when the Holy Spirit comes on you; and you will be my witnesses..." In Luke 9:1 Jesus gave the twelve "...power and authority to drive out all demons and to cure diseases..." In order for the followers of Christ to be effective they needed both the right and the ability to do the job.

All organizations need both authority and power to be effective. But the church is not an organization, it is an organism. This means that there is a Head, Jesus Christ, and a Body, which contains the cells which are His people.

In a local church we must recognize both power and authority. Roy M. Oswald in his booklet, "Power Analysis of a Congregation," makes a good distinction between the two terms. "*Authority* is granted the people by the system through roles to be occupied. *Power* relates to an individual's ability to accomplish things outside of, or over and above the authority given to them in roles."[3] Another way of stating the difference is that authority comes through the positions designated in the constitution and organizational structure of the church. Power is the ability to make decisions outside of this structure. In all churches there is the formal system (authority) and the informal system (power) that effect the decision making process. In most cases when there is a dispute, both sides or both parties have good intentions. But the decisions of a few people can determine the direction of the church, and sometimes its destiny as well.

Power is neither inherently good nor evil.[4] If those who use it are under the control of Jesus Christ, it can build up the church. If people who use power are not in submission to the Head of the church, it can become crippling or devastating. Power usually becomes necessary when those in authority are unwilling or unable to function. In other words, it often exists when there is a leadership vacuum. Paul M. Harrison in his book

Authority and Power In the Free Church Tradition comments about this dynamic in Baptist associations. "When Baptists eliminated bishops from their places they also eliminated the ecclesiastical authority of their own associations. The bishops returned in business suits to direct affairs from behind the curtain of the center stage."[5] No organization can function without leadership. When authority is eliminated, either anarchy prevails or those who have the wrong kind of power take over.

An excellent illustration of this dilemma is found in Jotham's fable about leadership, in Judges 9:8-15. The trees held a convention to select a king to rule over them. First they asked the olive tree and it declined. Then they asked the fig tree and it declined. Finally, they asked the vine and it declined. All of these represented the rightful legitimate heirs to the throne. Each was either too busy doing something else or did not see the importance of serving as a leader. Their attitude was "let someone else do it." Usually there is someone who is waiting and willing. In this fable it was the thornbush. The thornbush had no qualifications, no authority, and in this case no desire to help the trees. But, since no one else was available, the trees were willing to submit to its leadership. The thornbush took over and ultimately destroyed all the trees.

Power can be selfish and destructive. Or it can be the kind of power which is given to us by an omnipotent God through the power of the Holy Spirit.

Who Has Authority in the Church?

Before I discuss how and where power exists in ecclesiastical organizations, let us see where the church derives its authority. Although all churches and denominations claim to have their authority from the Scriptures, the organizational structures are often quite different from one another. Each group claims that there is one particular structure in the Scripture, after which its organization is modeled. Today, debate continues about whether or not we can adopt a particular form of church structure based on the pattern of the early church described in the book of Acts. Although there are basic principles set forth, we must remember the book of Acts is a transitional book where organizational patterns were emerging. We recognize that church systems developed historically and that the book of Acts can be viewed more as a descriptive document than a prescriptive one.

All churches and denominations have one of five basic church governmental structures. No one can hope to adjust the tension in the church between authority and power without understanding the uniqueness and the differences of each structure. They all relate to the source of authority. Dr. Roger Nicole, a seminary professor of mine at Gordon-Conwell Theological Seminary, clarified these systems for me. He drew a circle on the blackboard. Starting with the most authoritarian system at the top, he went counterclockwise on the circle to the least authoritarian system. By the time he got back to the top of the circle, the least authoritarian system was very close in practice to the most authoritarian.

The five church government structures are as follows. I have described them focusing on where the authority lies within each system.

1. *One Person Above the Local Church Has the Final Authority.* Often this system is called the hierarchical system and is associated with the Roman Catholic Church. The Pope is at the top of the pyramid and all control of the positions and property are ultimately in his hands. In the case of the Roman Catholic Church, this person resides outside of the influence and authority of a particular church. In Protestant churches this person may be the pastor who has acquired the final authority. He has the final decision about positions and may even

control the finances and own the property. Sometimes he or she may be considered a "benevolent dictator," but nevertheless he or she is a dictator. In one church on the East coast the moderator appoints the nominating committee and the nominating committee places only one name on the ballot for each office.

2. *A Few People Above the Local Church Have the Final Authority.* This system is called the episcopal system, and it has many similarities to the hierarchical system. Instead of the final authority being vested in one person, several people possess this power. These people may be called Bishops, Superintendents or members of the Council. They usually have the authority to ordain, appoint leadership in the local church and control the church's physical assets, including the property. Although the amount of authority they choose to exercise varies, very little happens without their approval or blessing.

3. *Many Persons Outside the Local Church Have the Final Authority.* Sometimes this system is called the synodical system. This system has one or more groups outside of the local church that have final authority over a church. A local group, a regional group and a national or international group may be included in the outside groups. Usually representatives from local churches are included. In fact, ministers usually are not members of local churches, but are members of the outside group. This group, such as a Presbytery or Synod, has authority to ordain, own property and to place or approve pastoral leadership in a local church.

4. *All the People Within the Local Church Have the Final Authority.* This system, characterized by the autonomy of the local church, is called the congregational form of government. Everyone who is a member of the congregation has equal voice and equal vote. No outside ecclesiastical group has any authority over the local church, although the local church may voluntarily decide to unite with an outside group. The membershi

of the local church owns the property and buildings, ordains and calls its own pastor. Many of these churches are associated with no ecclesiastical group outside of their church.

5. *A Few People Within the Local Church Have the Final Authority.* This system is sometimes referred to as the oligarchical system. In this system the leaders in the church may or may not be ordained ministers. Sometimes these individuals are called elders. But whatever the group is called, these individuals have the authority to control the direction and the functioning of the local church. They elect, appoint or remove leadership in the church. The congregation does not have the final authority, it merely approves the decisions of those in leadership. Quite often the small group that is in control is self-perpetuating and serves a lifetime term in office.

The governments of many denominations and local churches are a modification of one of these five systems, while some groups possess a combination of systems. The distinguishing factor in each is which person or group has the final authority to make decisions which effect the functioning of the church.

Authority is the right to act. One of the problems in local churches is that sometimes people who have been granted the right to act are unwilling or unable to act. When this happens, people outside the roles of authority make the decisions. They have the power. In other situations, those outside the system oppose those who have authority.

Who Has the Power?

Where do people in a church obtain the power to make decisions? There are four different sources of power that exist in a congregation.[6] Each has the ability to influence the congregation positively or negatively.

1. *Reputational Power.* These are people who by their charisma, money or position are able to influence or control others. People who belong to this group may or may not hold any official position in the church. In fact, they may not even be active in attendance. These individuals might be leading citizens in the community, holding office in the local government or perhaps an administrative position in the local school.

Other people with this kind of power can include the manager of a company that employs a number of people from the church. A few individuals may possess the money that is needed to make a particular program successful, and wield this influence as power. Another group of people whose reputation puts them in a place of power might include the former pastor or a former pastor's spouse who still lives in the community.

In fact, there are those who aren't even members of the church who are making decisions. When I worked as Placement Director at a seminary on the East Coast, we were contacted by a man who wanted us to send the names of pastoral candidates to him. He was a physician who lived in New York state. The church was in Vermont, and he attended there in the summer. He was screening all candidates and suggesting names to the church.

2. *Coalitional Power.* This is not solo power but group power. There are many subgroups in the church who have power because of the numbers of people they include. These subgroups may include an adult Sunday school class, the choir, the youth group, women's groups, men's groups, family groups, the softball team, or the nursery workers. The group may be organized or it may be quite informal.

In one church where I served there was a Bible study that met weekly. Although most of the people did not have leadership positions in the church, much discussion and many decisions were made at that meeting. Many such groups have n "official leader," but often the unofficial leader is the pers who talks the most about the fact that group doesn't have a leader.

3. *Communicational Power.* These are the persons who have access to information about congregational activities and about people within the congregation. They may control a formal network such as a prayer chain or church newsletter, or they may control an informal network because of their presence around the church. People in this latter category can include the secretary, the custodian, the organist or the retired person who helps around the church. These individuals can decide what information people hear and who will hear the information. The information they disseminate may be accurate or inaccurate, necessary or unnecessary, balanced or unbalanced. Just as newscasters on television and radio help to shape information and opinions, so do those that control information in the church networks.

4. *Structural Power.* These are the people who have official positions within the organization. They already have authority because of their positions. People who belong to this category are board members, financial officers, Sunday school superintendents, staff members and members of elected or appointed committees. If any system is to work effectively, those who have authority must be people of power. If those who have been called to lead don't lead, there is chaos and lack of direction.

Power will exist in each of these categories. The solution to the tension between authority and power is not to eliminate or shackle power, but to channel it so that the power helps fuel the organization rather than destroy it. Any tension adjustment must be skillfully performed so that those who have been given the authority do not let those who are unauthorized control the organization. On the other hand, those who have authority must be careful not to suppress the creativity and differences of those who have no authority. Maintaining this balance is not simple, but it is essential for the health and growth of a local church. Here are some suggestions which will facilitate the process.

Five Ways to Adjust the Tension

If You Have No Goals, Any Direction Will Get You There. One reason for many "power plays" in the church is that most people have no idea what the goals of the church are. To be meaningful, goals must be measurable, attainable and able to be owned. It is not enough for the senior pastor, the staff, or the official board to formulate and adopt the goals. If goals are *your* goals they may or may not be acceptable. Goals need to become *our* goals.

One way that goals become ownable and owned is by involving the entire congregation in an assessment process. Many people will not support anything that has been decided without their input. People have ideas and opinions which they need to express. On a couple of occasions the entire congregation where I served did an assessment. Leaders asked people to respond to three questions. "What are the strengths of the church?" (which means, what do you feel good about?). "What are the weaknesses of the church?" (what things don't you feel good about?). "What are your hopes and dreams for the church?" (what things would you like to see happen?). For more information of this process, consult the book by Lloyd Perry and Norman Shawchuck, *Revitalizing the Twentieth Century Church.*

During the process of assessment, people will indicate if they agree with the direction the church is heading. One way to determine if a person agrees with the direction of the church is to listen to how he refers to the church. Does he or she refer to the church as "we" or "they." If the church is "they," individuals still believe it is the leaders' church and not theirs.

The Process Is As Important As the Product. The church is not a business; it is a voluntary association. A church can be "businesslike," but we cannot make decisions in the same way that decisions are made in a business. Although making a decision may be more efficiently done by a few people in authority, a broader base of support increases the effectiveness of a decision. When communities and organizations are by-passed for the sake of efficiency, they may use their power to stifle progress. In a church you can't go from first base to third base without touching second.

People need to feel they are important if they are to be considered members. Participatory democracy does not mean that everyone is to be involved in making decisions, but everyone needs to feel that their input is important.

Involvement means more than attending worship service on Sunday and an occasional special event. When I had served as pastor of Temple Baptist for a couple of months, a young man made an appointment to see me. He wanted to know the church's purposes and goals. Every Sunday morning he and his family sat in the front row of the balcony looking around at everybody and everything. He never attended Sunday school, evening services, Bible studies during the week, or business meetings. He never volunteered to serve on a committee or to help with a project. He was not a participant. He was an "efficiency expert." An efficiency expert is someone from the outside who analyzes and examines an organization to make it run more efficiently. The way to find out about a church is to volunteer and get involved in its process.

Agree To Disagree Agreeably. Mrs. Billy Graham was once asked if she agreed with everything her husband said. She replied, "If two people agree on everything one of them isn't necessary." It is all right to disagree, even in your church.

We should not only tolerate differing feelings and opinions, but welcome them. People with a constant negative attitude, however, must not be given a constant forum and platform. Those who exhibit a critical spirit should not be allowed in leadership positions such as that of a teacher or board member.

Unity does not mean that we must have unanimity or uniformity or unison. Diversity is positive as long as there is agreement on purpose, goals and direction of the church.

More Important To Do the Right Thing Than To Be Right. Marshall Shelley in his book *Well-Intentioned Dragons* talks about people who use their authority to get their way. They abuse their power and demand their rights by vetoing programs, overruling pastors and changing directions of the church. "Churches can thus be victimized by people who see being 'right' as more important than being 'nice.' Those who make absolutes out of issues others see as negotiable can stymie the will of the majority."[7]

Most church differences are not centered around beliefs, but around procedures and personalities. When people start demanding their "rights" rather than doing the "right thing," an atmosphere of confrontation develops. We can learn and teach others the importance of an irenic spirit by example and from the Scriptures. An irenic spirit is something that can be both taught and caught.

Apollos is a good scriptural model of a person with an irenic spirit. In 1 Corinthians 1:10-11, the apostle Paul senses a division in the Corinthian church, based on personality. He appeals to them, ". . . in the name of our Lord Jesus Christ, that all of you agree with one another so that there may be no divisions among you. . . . One of you says, 'I follow Paul'; another, 'I follow Apollos'; another, 'I follow Cephas'; still another, 'I follow Christ.'"

Apollos was not willing to participate in this division. In

1 Corinthians chapter 16, verse 12, we read, "Now about our brother Apollos: I strongly urged him to go to you with the brothers. He was quite unwilling to go now, but he will go when he has the opportunity." I believe that Apollos was looking for the right chance to adjust the tension in the church at Corinth. He was a leader more concerned about doing the right thing than in seeking or demanding his rights.

Decide What To Go To the Wall For. "We can make our plans, but the final outcome is in God's hands. We can always 'prove' that we are right, but is the Lord convinced?" (Proverbs 16:1-2, *Living Bible*). One of the decisions that leaders need to make is, "What are you going to go to the wall for?" Gordon MacDonald, President of Inter-Varsity Christian Fellowship, used to tell seminary students that one of the greatest problems that many pastors have is going to the wall for the wrong things.

Many leaders have confused opinions with convictions. Whether the choir wears robes or doesn't wear robes, the scheduled time of a meeting, the kinds of seats in the sanctuary, the color of paint in the foyer, and the number of people on a committee, are a few of the issues that have become major battlegrounds in churches.

Going to the wall is usually a painful experience, but sometimes it is necessary. We can't compromise the fundamentals of our faith, moral purity or obedience to the laws of the land. Taking a stand is not popular, but being willing to "go to the wall" for the right things is essential.

Working creatively to adjust the tension between power and authority is both an art and a challenge. Although Jesus Christ was strong, He possessed a meek spirit. Meekness is not weakness. In the words of Dr. Earl Radmacher of Western Baptist Seminary, "If you think meekness is weakness, you try to be meek for a week."

Power is neither good nor bad, and it cannot be eliminated.

Certain people in any group have leadership ability. A tension adjuster will discover those who possess leadership gifts and prod them on to develop their skills. A tension adjuster will encourage these people and try to provide opportunities for them to use their leadership abilities. Hopefully, your church will recognize people who possess power and put them in places of authority.

After identifying people and groups who have power, the church needs to establish effective and accurate communication with these people. This can be done both verbally and in written form. If people are not given a forum to express their ideas and use their gifts, they will become counterproductive or indifferent.

Spiritual unity is maintained when those in authority are trained how to use their positions to lead in a positive, productive direction.

Footnotes

1. Campolo, Anthony Jr., *The Power Delusion* (Wheaton, IL: Victor Books, 1983), p. 76.

2. Campolo, p. 11.

3. Oswald, Roy M., "Power Analysis of a Congregation" (Washington, D.C.: The Alban Institute, Inc., 1981), p. 7.

4. Campolo, p. 14.

5. Harrison, Paul M., *Authority and Power In the Free Church Tradition* (Princeton, NJ: Princeton University Press, 1959), p. 227.

6. Oswald, pp. 9-10.

7. Shelley, Marshall, *Well-Intentioned Dragons* (Waco, TX: Word Books, 1985), p. 67.

6

"I'm Independent"

The Tension Between Independency and Denominationalism

It was the first day of a homiletics class I was taking in graduate school with Professor Faris Whitesell. The class was made up of students who had come from a variety of educational institutions. Each one of us, when our name was called, was to identify our denominational background. "Kerr, what are you?" "Presbyterian," he replied. "Hough, what is your denomination?" "Assembly of God," he answered. "Didier, what's your background?" "Baptist," he responded. "Prinzing, what are you?" "Independent," I said hesitantly. "Independent of what? Everybody and everything?" the professor asked poignantly. Everyone in the room, except me, had a good laugh. The discussion changed to other topics, but the implication of being an "independent" became a constant concern to me.

All my life I had been an independent. My parents had helped organize an independent church in a Chicago suburb. From the time I was old enough, I attended camps at independent conference grounds. When it came time to go to high school

I traveled fourteen miles from home to study at an independent Christian school. After graduation I spent four years attending independent Christian colleges. Then I studied three more years at an independent seminary. Our church supported independent "faith missions" exclusively.

My growing-up years took place during the midst of the modernist-fundamentalist controversy. There were many differences among people who called themselves independents, but the one thing that all independent churches had in common was their opposition to denominations. Denomination was a "four letter word" synonymous with being apostate. Belonging to a denomination was not as bad as belonging to a Roman Catholic Church, but it ranked a close second.

Back in the '40s and '50s we considered ourselves anti-denominational. By the middle '50s we no longer saw denominations as a threat. As we began to be more and more comfortable with our own identity we began to refer to ourselves as *un-* or *non*-denominational. By the 1960s, studies by religious researchers Stark and Glock indicated that people were switching to the more liberal denominational groups. As they saw it, "Liberal churches were appealing for two reasons: one, because of upward social mobility in American society and the tendency for the upwardly mobile to switch to more liberal higher status churches; and second, because many people out of theological conviction were finding the demythologized beliefs of the liberal churches more congruent with modern life . . . liberal churches at the time were enjoying a great deal of respectability and appeared on the surface at least as healthy as growing institutions."[1] Some independent churches and independent Christian colleges and seminaries began to refer to themselves as *inter*-denominational in the 1950s in order to be accepted by denominations.

By the end of 1950s, when it was time for me to graduate from seminary and become the pastor of a local church, I had to decide what I was. "Prinzing, what are you?" became more than a question of information or academic discussion. It became a real issue.

For the first time, I had to face squarely the tension between denominationalism and independency. The more I studied the more I became convinced that the early church was not independent but *inter-dependent*. Although I wasn't sure whether I was ready to cooperate with denominational churches, I was certain that I wanted to cooperate with other evangelical churches. After being independent all of my life, I felt I should be able to associate with some group of churches.

The Source of the Problem

The tension between independency and denominations is not one that only seminary students face. It also must be faced at other times and in other settings.

Newly organized churches must decide if they are going to be independent or affiliate with a group of churches. Churches that are independent need to consider if they are going to become part of a denomination. And churches that are part of a denomination need to consider whether they want to become independent. Pastors and members are faced with a decision if they are going to switch denominations or switch from a denominational affiliation to an independent church, or vice versa.

For most people, the choice between denominationalism and independency is not simply a matter of preference, but stems from a theological conviction. The issue behind the two choices centers around one's view of the ecumenical movement. The word ecumenical comes from the Greek *oikoumene*, which means the whole inhabited earth. Those who supported the recent ecumenical movement believe in the visible unity of the organized church. The key verse for the movement came from the Lord's Prayer in John 17:21, ". . . that all of them may be one, Father, just as you are in me and I am in you. May they also be in us so that the world may believe that you have sent me."

The liberal wing of Christianity spawned the concept of ecumenism. Most of the large denominations supported this movement. They viewed the schisms, divisions and an independent spirit as contrary to the scriptural teaching of unity. In August 1948 the World Council of Churches was organized and in November of 1950 the National Council of Churches came into existence. For many denominations the ecumenical movement was not only a logical conclusion of their theological position but also a direction to which they were committed.

On the other hand, the independent found his identity in Scripture as well. Like those of a more liberal persuasion, the independent sought for unity among God's people. However, the unity did not come from a visibly organized church, but was an invisible spiritual unity based on a oneness in Christ. Instead of the emphasis being primarily on oneness, it centered around separateness. A key verse for independents is 2 Corinthians 6:17, "Therefore, come out from them and be *separate*, says the Lord. Touch no unclean thing and I will receive you." Any oneness that was not based on the fundamentals of the faith (infallibility of Scripture, virgin birth, substitutionary atonement, bodily resurrection, visible return) was considered to be unacceptable. Most independents felt strongly about both the fundamentals of Scripture and separateness from the ecumenical movement.

For many Christians and churches, the battle lines were drawn and the walls were erected. Those who were affiliated with most of the mainline denominations were part of the "ecumenical movement." Those who were affiliated with an independent church were part of the "separatist movement." Was it possible to cooperate with other churches who were not from your local church and be a member of an independent church? Was it possible for churches to remain in a denomination and not be associated with the ecumenical movement? This was the tension that many faced and continue to face.

In the late 1950s there was an uneasiness among many people with the extreme separatist position and its rejection of any type of visible unity among churches. Some became known as "fighting fundamentalists." Fundamentalism had become descriptive of their attitude rather than their position. One particular group that I had contact with used to ask who your enemies were. Then, if your enemies matched up with its enemies, the people would have fellowship with you. It was impossible for them ". . . to contend for the faith that was once for all entrusted to the saints" without being contentious.

If the tension between denominationalism and independency is to be properly adjusted, we need to restudy various terms. One is the term "ecumenism." A second is the term "evangelical," and a third is "denomination." J. Marcellus Kik in his book *Ecumenism and the Evangelical* attempted to redefine the term "ecumenism" so that those who believed in the fundamentals of the faith could accept it. "Ecumenical is the movement in the universal, visible church upon earth by which, under the influence and guidance of the Holy Spirit, the church comes into the unity of the faith and of the knowledge of the Son of God, into the measure of the stature of the fullness of Christ."[2] Can evangelicals accept that definition? Maybe it is more important to redefine or at least define the word evangelical? It's amazing how the meaning of words can change over the years. An evangelical, according to Kik, has historically been designated as "one who holds to the absolute supremacy of Scripture as a rule of faith and practice, and to justification by free grace by faith."[3]

An Issue of Biblical Unity

As evangelicals, we need to decide if unity among believers is to be expressed in any visible way. What is the difference between unity, unification, uniformity and unanimity? Is it possible to spend an eternity with the people in heaven that we have decided to separate ourselves from on earth? Examine the meaning of the word unity in John 17:21, Ephesians 4:3 and 4:13, in light of the sin of division and disunity that is evident among evangelicals today.

I don't intend to gloss over the many difficulties that are raised over what unity is and how it is to be accomplished. Martyn Lloyd-Jones, the great expository preacher from England, comments, "It is a tragedy that division ever entered the life of the church. In addition, we must all regard schism as grievous sin. That is common ground. But having said that, one must also point out that there is obviously great confusion and much disagreement as to what constitutes unity, and to how unity is to be obtained and preserved."[4]

Unfortunately, many people view separation and isolation synonymously. Believers need to practice separation unto God, separation from the world, but not separation from one another. One of the most difficult tasks for evangelicals today is learning how much separation is good and with whom do we fellowship. In an issue of the newsletter of MARC, a ministry of World Vision, there is an excellent insight on this subject of cooperation. "One of the most difficult things in the world for us to do in the religious world is to cooperate. For those of us who are Westerners, our total life experience predisposes us against cooperation, breeds competition and makes us suspicious of others. . . . History shows that the West began an almost insurmountable tendency to apply a long series of rational theological tests to everything and everybody as preconditions to working together. . . . Our attitudes exaggerate

the Scriptural admonition to separation and purity, and on too frequent occasions, they fly in the face of the biblical call to unity."[5]

Biblical unity does not come from human incentive. The basis of Christian unity is based on the person and work of Jesus Christ as revealed in the Word of God. Unity does not start with either ministry or fellowship. It must begin with a oneness of belief. There can be no unity apart from the Head of the Body. It cannot be produced by conferences, creeds, confessions or dialogues.

It is not difficult to accept and understand unity from a vertical standpoint — the believer's unity with Christ. There is no unity apart from the reality of a relationship in Christ. Theologian Dr. G. W. Bromiley emphasizes that the relationship with Christ is more than a declaration or a legal statement, or some type of goal or kind of idealism.[6] If the world is to know that believers are one, we must have both a vertical unity and an horizontal unity if we are to function as an organism. In order to demonstrate that there is a oneness in Christ, biblical ecumenism must transcend denominational, racial, economic, ethnic and geographical barriers.

Eroding Allegiance to Denominations

Among many evangelicals the term denomination creates negative vibrations. Where did this term come from? What did it mean? What does it mean today?

Historically, denominations were visible expressions of groups of churches which had common beliefs, objectives and purposes. These churches banded together because they desired to make unity a reality. Over the years denominations became powerful organizations that lost their identity and purpose. The intention was good, but in many cases the vitality was missing. Denominationalism became the scapegoat for many ills in the church. Some of the criticism was justified, much of it was not.

Many people who used to spend time delivering tirades against denominations, now have turned to more pressing issues. A newer term describing a person's relationship to denominations has emerged. Some churches have begun using the phrase *trans-denomination* to describe their church's position. These churches consider themselves to have journeyed beyond the need for or the threat of denominations.

There has been a significant decline in denominational allegiance during the past decade. Switching denominations or affiliating with independent churches has become a sign of the time. People today switch loyalties in many areas of life. Changing schools, political parties, and places where they shop are considered a way of life.

Lyle Schaller, in an article titled "Erosion of Denominational Loyalty," gives many factors that have contributed to this decline:

1. Increase in interdenominational and interfaith marriages
2. Ecumenical movement
3. Increase in social and economic mobility
4. Denominational mergers
5. Nondenominational para-church groups
6. Charismatic Renewal
7. Ministers not trained in denominational seminaries
8. National climate of anti-institutionalism
9. Decline in emphasis on missions and camp by denominations
10. Decline of children of church members going to denominational schools
11. Decline in members who subscribe to denominational magazines
12. Merger of theological seminaries[7]

Those who view denominations negatively see them as archaic, devisive and irrelevant. On the other hand, those who view independents negatively see them as devisive, uncooperative and self-centered. Denominationalism and independency appear to be dramatically opposed. The proper adjustment of this tension does not eliminate either extreme. All members of denominations should not become independents any more than all members of independent churches should change their allegiance to a denominational church.

The Key to Adjusting This Tension

The key to adjusting the tension between denominationalism and independency is a mutual agreement on the necessity of *cooperation* among God's people. If the world is to know that believers are one, we must have both an invisible unity as well as some type of visible unity. That unity will be expressed horizontally in some type of cooperation. In order to demonstrate that we have oneness in Christ, biblical ecumenism must transcend denominational, racial, economic, ethnic and geographical barriers.

On the other hand, if we need to compromise our convictions in order to join together, we will not be effective. Walls, fences and barriers are needed if we are to maintain doctrinal convictions in the church. Cooperation requires recognition of differences between churches and an understanding of distinctives. The walls that separate Christians, however, are to be different types of barriers than the ones that separate Christian and non-Christian groups. In Ephesians 2:14 we read that, ". . .he himself is our peace, who has made the two one and has destroyed the barrier, the dividing wall of hostility." Any walls that we construct among Christians should not be permanent. They should be movable partitions.

The story is told of a soldier who was killed during a battle in a small village in France. His buddies wanted him to have a proper burial. There was only one cemetery in town and that one was fenced in, adjacent to the Roman Catholic Church. They knocked on the door of the church and the priest came and asked what they wanted. "Our buddy just died and we would like to give him a proper burial. Could we have permission to bury him in your cemetery?" they asked. When the priest found out that their dead buddy was not of the Roman Catholic faith, he had no choice. He was bound by his ecclesiastical rules to forbid their request. That afternoon the soldiers dug a shallow grave and buried their friend just outside the fence.

The following morning they came to put some flowers on the grave, but couldn't find the grave site. The soldiers went back to the church and knocked on the door. When the priest came, they asked him if he knew what had happened to their buddy's grave site. "Last night I went outside and moved the fence so that the grave is now inside the cemetery," he replied. Whether we are part of a denominational church, or an independent church, cooperation may mean moving some fences.

Each church decides *with whom* to cooperate and also in *what* areas they will work together. No cooperation based on compromise of conviction will strengthen either the local church or the universal church. Cooperation among churches is biblically based. In Philippians 1:27 Paul exhorts the church at Philippi. "Only let your manner of life be worthy of the gospel of Christ, so that whether I come and see you or am absent, I may hear of you that you stand firm in one spirit, with one mind striving side by side for the faith of the gospel" (RSV). Paul was speaking to believers who have a oneness in Christ. He was prompting them not only to take a stand for what they believe, but also work together. They were to strive *with*, not *against*, their brethren. Evidently there were some who had lost sight of the enemy and were attacking each other. We see this in Phil. 1:15-17 and 4:1-4. This type of striving was contrary to Christ's command in John 13:34-35: "A new command I give you: Love one another. As I have loved you, so you must love one another. All men will know that you are my disciples if you love one another."

One of the paragraphs of the Lausanne Covenant, entitled "Cooperation in Evangelism," underscores this New Testament emphasis of cooperation.

> "We affirm that the church's visible unity in truth is God's purpose. Evangelism also summons us to unity because our oneness strengthens our witness, just as our disunity undermines our gospel of reconciliation. We recognize, however, that organizational unity may take many forms and does not necessarily forward evangelism. Yet we who share the same biblical faith should be closely united in fellowship, work, and witness. We confess that our testimony has sometimes been marred by sinful individualism and needless duplication. We pledge ourselves to seek a deeper unity in truth, worship, holiness and mission. We urge the development of regional and functional cooperation for the furtherance of the church's mission, for strategic planning, for mutual encouragement, and for the sharing of resources and experience."[8]

Ways to Cooperate

If your church is at a decision point, considering whether or not to affiliate with a denomination or to work with other churches, the question you need to answer is not, "Are we going to cooperate with anybody?" but, "At what level and in what areas are we going to cooperate?" Here are three levels of cooperation that your church should consider:

1. *Level of Affiliation*

At this level, there is some type of organizational or structural unity. Structural unity may take many forms depending on the form of government of the local church and the denomination. Independent churches who recognize each church's individual autonomy also may group themselves together in associations or fellowships of churches.

Affiliating with other churches allows the local church "to do together what each church cannot do by itself." Some of the ministries and activities that only a few "super churches" can do by themselves are: maintain schools, run camping programs, support a worldwide missions program, endorse chaplains, train pastors and missionaries, develop and produce Christian education and training materials.

Your affiliation may be on a local basis only. Or it might also be regional, national, or international. Whatever the type of affiliation your church enters into, that affiliation is to help encourage the local church in its purpose to glorify God through worship, evangelism and edification.

2. *Level of Celebration*

In a small town in New England, there were three churches in the community: a Roman Catholic church, a Unitarian church, and an evangelical church, of which I was the interim pastor. The Unitarian pastor invited me to speak at the Roman Catholic church in a combined Thanksgiving service. The elders of the evangelical church refused to cooperate because they realized that next year it would be someone else's turn to preach in our church. If you don't agree on the person and work of Christ, how can you participate in celebration?

A local church may not choose to affiliate with other churches in an association of churches or denomination, but can still participate in joint worship services. Although views about the Word of God, work of God, and the worship of God can not be compromised, the emphasis in these meetings needs to be placed on areas of agreement, not on the many differences that exist. This includes the choice of music, the selection of speakers and the nature of the program.

Another form of celebration is cooperative evangelistic efforts, especially in citywide rallies. Such efforts, whether they are for an extended period of time or held periodically, are visible signs of unity as well as evangelistic thrusts into the community. Trust the judgment of your spiritual leaders when considering whether or not to participate in joint event. You and everyone else have the freedom to refrain from participation for biblical reasons.

3. *Level of Demonstration*

Our participation together to meet community needs and concerns is much broader than is possible in the areas of worship and evangelism. Our motivation should be the same in either area, but our outward demonstration may be different. We can cooperate in acts of justice and morality on a wider scale than we can participate together in an Easter Sunrise Service or an evangelistic crusade.

Demonstrating our faith through social action is one way that churches can visibly show their desire to cooperate. Many churches are reticent to join together in this area because they fear being accused of preaching the social gospel, or of compromising their theological convictions. Although there are necessary cautions, morality is an area where the church must be "light" and "salt" without compromising its convictions.

A combined effort by many churches taking a stand against immorality in the community will have much greater impact than if an individual church stands by itself. Boycotting, letter writing and picketing are useful tools in taking stands against such evils as prostitution, abortion and pornography. It's not enough, however, for churches to be against immorality; they need to work together to provide alternatives to the victims, such as crisis pregnancy centers and places for prostitutes to live. In many communities there are an increasing number of street people. We need to continue to work together to support places such as rescue missions that minister to alcoholics and to drifters.

Another area where we need to cooperate is in the area of human resources. There are many people who need our help that are not victims of immorality, but of society. Some of these people are the elderly, poor, handicapped and the unemployed. One large evangelical church in Portland, Oregon, organized a people bank with the members of churches in their areas. Those in need could call a central number to get help with painting, moving, electrical work, plumbing, etc.

A final area where we can cooperate is in supporting justice. Many people are in danger of losing some of their basic rights and freedoms unless legal and conciliation services are made available. Although there are secular agencies providing this type of service, our churches need to show our Christian concern. Churches are to be instruments of peace. We can demonstrate this first by our love for one another. If people see division and strife within our churches, our attempts to be peacemakers will be diminished if not thwarted. We should both preach and practice reconciliation between people. We can pray for peace, teach it in the community and around the world, without becoming political activists. We are called to be peacemakers as representatives of the Prince of Peace.

Our Ministry of Reconciliation

In a world that is divided, the local church must do everything possible to bring unity. Biblical unity that comes from Jesus Christ. He has committed the ministry of reconciliation to us.

No longer can churches justify an uncooperative spirit with other churches. The degree and the extent of cooperation is left up to each church, including yours. Dr. G. W. Bromiley comments, "We may not agree what the church is or what kind of unity it ought to have, or what are the conditions of its attainment or how it is to be sought, but we all agree that the church ought to be one, and therefore that there ought to be some kind of ecumenical movement in a divided Christendom."[9] Some of us are members of local churches which belong to a denomination. Others belong to churches which do not have any denominational affiliation. All of us need to seek out ways of cooperation.

Not every church will feel free to affiliate at the denominational level. But every church should be able to cooperate with other churches in celebration and social action. Peacemakers are not passive or indifferent about their role. They seek out ways to cooperate with others.

Dr. Criswell, Pastor of the First Baptist Church, Dallas, Texas, tells the story about a farmer who discovered his little girl was missing. On all sides of his home there were wheat fields that were ready to be harvested. He tried desperately to call his daughter, but there was no answer. The next day people from other farms and from a nearby town came to help find the girl. They called her name and looked all over, but to no avail. The next day someone suggested that everyone hold hands and walk together through the fields. After a couple of hours, a man stumbled on the lifeless form of the little girl. He picked her up and ran carrying her in his arms to the father. When the father realized the child was dead, he thanked the people and said, "It's too bad we didn't join hands sooner; maybe my daughter would still be alive."

Pastor Martin Niemohler, a Protestant clergyman during the Nazi regime in Germany, reflected on his stand to be independent during those terrible days of oppression. "In Germany, the Nazis came for the Communists and I didn't speak up because I was not a Communist. Then they came for the Jews and I did not speak up because I was not a Jew. Then they came for the trade unionists and I didn't speak up because I wasn't a trade unionist. Then they came for the Catholics and I was a Protestant, so I didn't speak up. Then they came for me...by that time there was no one to speak for anyone."

"Prinzing, what are you?" Maybe it's not too late for those of us who claim to be part of God's family to begin joining hands. Let the mind of Christ be in you: "By this all men will know that you are my disciples, if you love one another."

Footnotes

1. Roof, Wade C. and Hadaway, Christopher K., "Denominational Switching In the Seventies: Going Beyond Stark and Glock," *Journal for the Scientific Study of Religion,* Vol. 18 No. 4, December 1979, pp. 363, 364.

2. Kik, J. Marcellus, *Ecumenism and The Evangelical* (Philadelphia: The Presbyterian and Reformed Publishing Company, 1958), p. 3.

3. *Ibid.* p. V.

4. Lloyd-Jones, Martyn, *The Basis of Christian Unity* (Grand Rapids, MI: Eerdmans, 1962), p. 5.

5. *MARC* Newsletter, January 1985, Monrovia, CA, World Vision International, p. 4.

6. Bromiley, G. W., *The Unity and Disunity of The Church* (Grand Rapids, MI: Eerdmans, 1963), p. 44.

7. Schaller, Lyle, "The Erosion of Denominational Loyalty," *The Parish Paper* Vol. 15, No. 4, October 1985.

8. "Cooperating in World Evangelization," Lausanne Occasional Papers, Number 24, Wheaton, IL, 1983, p. 9.

9. Bromiley, p. 14.

7

Throwing Gospel Bombs

The Tension Between Evangelism and the Social Gospel

In the Chicago suburb where I grew up, everyone had a place to live and enough food to eat. The only people who seemed to be lacking the basic necessities of food and shelter were those people who occasionally invaded our neighborhood. We called these intruders "bums," "hobos," or "tramps." None lived permanently in our community. Most rode the trains around the country. While they were in town they lived in abandoned shacks near the railroad tracks.

Occasionally, when they were very hungry, they would go from door-to-door begging for food. When they came to our house my mother always gave them a gospel tract, and sometimes a meal. (Everyone who came to our door, without exception, received a tract.) Since only a few of them came to our house, my mother felt that we should take the gospel to the rest of them. On Saturday afternoons she and I would go looking for tramps who were walking alongside the road. My mother drove and I sat in the back seat. She gave me a box full of "gospel bombs" — tracts which told people they were going to hell if they weren't saved. These tracts were wrapped tightly with colored cellophane and held together with a string.

When we spotted a tramp, Mom told me to throw a "gospel bomb" at his feet. (It wasn't against the law to litter in those days.) Then he was supposed to pick it up, realize he was a sinner going to hell, kneel down by the side of the road and ask Jesus Christ to come into his life. After throwing several gospel bombs, the challenge was gone. I decided to change my tactics to be more in keeping with my athletic skills. Instead of throwing them at the feet of the tramps, I tried to hit them in the head. Maybe a few became Christians through this evangelistic endeavor, but I doubt I'll meet anyone in heaven who found Christ through my pitching skills.

Should my mother and I have taken food to the tramps or thrown "gospel bombs" at them? Which did they need the most? If we didn't tell them about Jesus Christ, how would they learn about Him?

All of us probably would agree that the tramps along the highway needed both physical and spiritual food. But are both of these needs the responsibility of the church? And if they are, which comes first...the evangelism, or responding to social needs?

A tension that has surfaced in every church that I have been associated with has been the tension between evangelism and social ministry. The kind of social needs that churches face have changed, but the issue is still the same. A generation ago the main social concern that people struggled with in most communities was what to do about the alcoholic and the drifter. People who were found guilty of deviant practices were placed in jails or sent to other institutions.

Today most churches are faced with different social concerns in their communities, such as unemployment, inadequate housing, alcoholism and a host of other issues. Few communities have escaped the invasion of drugs, venereal disease, homosexuality, prostitution and abortion. By taking a stand against the social evils of the day, we have forgotten the victims of these who are involved — the drug addict, the homosexual, the prostitute and the unwed mother.

Although many of the social problems we read about in the Scriptures are not the same ones we face today, Jesus and the apostles gave us a good example to follow. They faced the same tension between ministering to a person's body and ministering to his soul.

How Jesus Faced this Tension

In John 5, we see Jesus going to a place where the social outcasts of society were gathered. There, at Bethesda, He was confronted by a great number of disabled people. Some were blind, others lame or paralyzed. One man who had been an invalid for 38 years may have given up hope of being cured. Jesus met the man's physical and spiritual needs simultaneously when he challenged the man to "Get up! Pick up your mat and walk."

The next recorded miracle that Jesus performed was on the shore of the Sea of Galilee. A crowd of 5,000 men plus women and children followed Him. Their immediate need was physical. They were hungry. He fed them all. Although the Bible says nothing about Him preaching to them at that time, through His prayer and the ensuing miracle He used the occasion to arouse their interest and hunger for spiritual bread.

In John 8, we see how Jesus dealt with a woman who had committed a capital offense — the sin of adultery. Quite possibly some of the men standing there were guilty of the same crime. If they hadn't committed adultery physically, they may have done so in their hearts. After contending with those who were judging her, Jesus dealt with the woman's spiritual need.

She had sinned and Jesus confronted her with her need to change.

Jesus encountered a blind man (see John 9). The disciples believed that the root of this man's problem was sin in his life. Although the man was a sinner, his blindness was not the result of any sin that either he or his parents had committed. As the man trusted in Jesus and obeyed His commands, he was healed both spiritually and physically.

There seems to be no obvious pattern in the way that Jesus ministered to people. Whether the person was blind, deaf, mute, crippled, demon possessed, diseased, leprous, or an outcast of society, Jesus always met the social need with action. Sometimes he met the spiritual need first, other times the physical need first. At times He met them simultaneously. On some occasions He presented the gospel to them, and at other times He did not. But He never turned anyone away.

After the ascension His apostles faced the same tensions. Following the outpouring of the Holy Spirit, Peter and John faced this tension. In Acts 3, we read about a beggar at the gate of the temple. Every day the crippled man was placed at the gate. The apostles could have avoided him. They could have met his immediate need for sustenance and neglected his real need. It was obvious that the man was both crippled and destitute. Peter and John ministered to both the man's physical and spiritual need. They healed him "in the name of Jesus Christ." The man ended up walking, jumping and praising God.

Neither you nor I will probably perform any miraculous healings like those of Jesus and the apostles. These are dramatic examples of blending evangelism and social ministry. So James puts the tension in perspective for us (James 2:15,16). "Suppose a brother or sister is without clothes and daily food. If one of you says to him, 'Go, I wish you well; keep warm and well fed,' but does nothing about his physical needs, what good is it?" Churches cannot ignore the tension between evangelism and social ministry.

In the minds of many Christians, these two emphases are synonymous. In the minds of others, they are diametrically opposed. In the early 1900s, advocates of the "social gospel" taught that good works were synonymous with the gospel. Their message was that evangelism simply was doing good to others. It is obvious that our social concern must be translated into social action. In James 2:18 we read, "But someone will say, 'You have faith; I have deeds.' Show me your faith without deeds, and I will show you my faith by what I do."

Five Common Views of Social Ministry

Today, evangelicals who basically agree on the fundamentals of the faith cannot agree on their approach to meeting the social needs of mankind, or if or how this relates to evangelism. There are several approaches. Leighton Ford, vice president of Billy Graham Evangelistic Association, has categorized five different ways evangelicals see their social responsibility.[1]

1. *As a Distraction From Evangelism.* People who hold this view see their primary mandate as reaching a lost world for Jesus Christ. The Great Commission is clear and the time is short. Reaching the greatest number of people for Christ in the shortest amount of time is on the top of their agendas.

Spending time with any type of social ministry clouds the issue and diverts their efforts toward world evangelization. One preacher described this sentiment in these terms: "Jesus did not come to take people out of slums, but slums out of people." In this view, Jesus was not primarily concerned about the least and the last, but the lost.

2. *As a Result of Evangelism.* People who espouse this view see social ministry as the outcome of evangelism. If people's lives are changed inwardly they will have the desire and the ability to change their circumstances outwardly. "Changed people will change the world." Social parasites are able to become

social contributors.

Although all men aren't created equal physically, all men are created equal in Christ. In this view, people in the ghettos and slums who have inadequate housing and are unemployed will, with the help of the Holy Spirit, be able to change their condition in life.

3. *As a Preparation For Evangelism.* Proponents of this view believe that "hungry people will not listen to sermons." When people's basic needs are unmet, they are not interested in anything you say, but only in what you are able to do. Once they have the necessities of food, clothing and shelter, they will listen to the gospel. There is no hunger and thirst after righteousness as long as there is a struggle for survival.

As a result of this view, mammoth relief projects are planned. Sending people who will teach the lost about agriculture, education, sanitation and medicine becomes a prime concern. "Once we change the world, we will be able to change the people."

4. *As a Partner of Evangelism.* Those who believe this to be the biblical perspective see the "teachings of Jesus as always being accompanied by deeds of mercy and justice." In order to row a boat you must have two oars in the water — faith and works. If you are only using one you are basically going around in circles. These become the twin objectives of the church and always must be kept in balance.

5. *As An Essential Element of Evangelism.* People who hold to this view believe that the whole gospel must be presented to the whole person. Witnessing must be seen as an "inseparable whole which includes both proclamations and works of social justice." The ministry of reconciliation comes through both word and deeds. Social ministry and evangelism are inseparable attempts to bring the whole gospel to the whole person.

The approaches that churches use to attempt to balance the tension between evangelism and social ministry vary. Most are based on one of these five interpretations of what the Bible teaches.

Motivated By Love

It is clear from Scripture that Christian faith can never be separated from Christian social responsibility. Whatever we do must be motivated by a love for people which is based upon the love of Christ. In Mark 9:41, Jesus told His disciples, "I tell you the truth, anyone who gives you a cup of water in my name because you belong to Christ will certainly not lose his reward."

We are commanded to reach out to those who are in need in the world. If we are to preach the whole gospel, we must understand that the Great Commission and the Great Commandment must be tied together by the Great Compassion. The Great Commission found in Matthew 28:18-20 emphasizes our "going." As people under obligation, we must go. Likewise, social ministry must not be seen as something we do because we feel like doing it, but because we must do it. Inspiration is preceded by obligation. It is rarely very exciting to work with the filthy and poor of society.

A church in the San Diego area has a tremendous ministry to young people who come from affluent homes. Many of the young people they reach are heavily involved in drugs. After they become Christians these young people are asked to testify of their faith in Christ to their peers, and are taken to Tijuana, Mexico, where they spend a day at an orphanage. Instead of preaching to the children there, they clean the latrines and comb the lice out of the children's hair.

In Mark 12:28, one of the teachers of the law asked Jesus a very crucial question, "Of all the commandments, which is the most important?" The most important one, Jesus answered,

". . . is this: 'Hear, O Israel, the Lord our God, the Lord is one. Love the Lord your God with all your heart and with all your soul and with all your mind and with all your strength.' The second is this: 'Love your neighbor as yourself.' There is no commandment greater than these." *Doing* must not be separated from *loving*.

Outwardly, the social involvement of Christians resembles the efforts of their humanistic neighbors in the community. The difference between the Christian and the humanist is that the Christian is motivated by the love of Christ and the humanist is not. A Christian also has the spiritual resources available which help him or her to meet the total needs of the person.

Are the preaching and practice of your church consistent? Is your concern translated into action? Dr. Horace L. Fenton, former director of Latin America Missions, warns, "If the church shirks her duty to show the application of the Christian faith to the social needs of men, she does it at the expense of the good name of Christ in the world. It is all too possible for an individual believer to fail to see the connection between his love for God and his responsibility to his fellow man, unless it is pointed out to him—not just once, but many times. To expect the Holy Spirit to do this apart from the church, which is His chosen instrument, is a hope which finds no basis in either Scripture or Christian experience."[2]

What Is Your Plan?

Each local church must have a strategy to adjust the tension between evangelism and social responsibility in its own community as well as in other parts of the world.

Many churches have not identified their community or targeted the groups within their community. People are mobile in all areas of their life. Children no longer go to neighborhood schools, wives no longer shop at the neighborhood store, men no longer work at the neighborhood factory, and families no longer worship at the neighborhood church.

It's difficult to identify with both communities — where the church is located and where its members live. A church must meet the needs of people in the area where the church building is located. It's much easier to have a concern for people in other areas while neglecting the people in our own area. Your church needs to examine its own community, define the boundaries and identify the target groups in the area.

Temple Baptist Church in Portland, Oregon was organized 100 years ago to minister to Scandinavian immigrants who had come to the Northwest. Not only did the community change, but also the ministry needs. The immigration of Europeans slowed to a trickle. The residential area around the church changed to a commercial area. Few families stayed in the community.

Both from the pulpit and in small groups we stood against the evils of the day. Our total involvement both in evangelism and social ministry was through supporting rescue missions on the other side of the river. Every month we took charge of an evening meeting at one of the rescue mission centers.

Our community changed, even though the building remained at the same location. People who surrounded the church were of two kinds. First, there were office workers and shoppers who lived throughout the city. The second kind of people was not as visible. They were the transients, elderly, mentally handicapped and prostitutes. All of them had tremendous needs. Our church desired to be evangelistic, but our immediate neighborhood didn't seem to have very good prospects, so we looked beyond our community. As many churches have done, we began a bus ministry. We brought in hundreds of children to the church from many places all over the city. For the most part, few if any of our people lived in these areas.

Children heard the gospel message and many of them made decisions. But we made very little contact with the communities or the families where these people lived. Many of the social needs of these families were obvious. The bus workers did what they could, but the church was not committed to ministering to these families or identifying with these communities. After the initial excitement wore down, very few children continued to attend the church. No families from the bus ministry were assimilated into the life of the church.

Bus ministries have proved to be very successful in many places, but they did not help us to adjust the tension between evangelism and social ministry. We needed to identify the people in the community around our church. Then we needed to target the different groups of people and develop a strategy to meet their physical and spiritual needs.

When we first faced people who were socially unacceptable — prostitutes, transients and the handicapped — we were uncomfortable with their presence in the community. In the case of the prostitutes, we felt that even having them around was a detriment to maintaining a wholesome environment for our youth.

It was not until we began to love these people, who were society's victims, that God gave us a ministry with them. Whether or not any of them ever became Christians or attended our church, we wanted to love them through Christ. As we expressed our love, they responded. Not in spectacular numbers, but in significant individual changes. Some became Christians, others changed their lifestyles and became productive members of society.

Should all churches adopt this kind of ministry? Definitely not! There are very few situations where the circumstances and the needs are the same. Each church must find creative ways to become involved in both evangelism and social ministry in its community. Social ministry and evangelism must never be placed in a position of either/or, but both/and.

Two Ways We May Be One-Sided

If our social concern is to be effective, it must be followed by social action. Unless Christians are willing to get involved in the lives of people who have these problems, the gospel message remains one-sided. On the other hand, helping people out of their predicament without giving them an opportunity to put something else in its place is also one-sided. Jesus not only preached against sin in the case of the Samaritan woman, but He also helped her to find a better life.

As Christians, we are exhorted to be both salt and light. If this is going to become a reality for the church, the emphasis must not be on a monastic withdrawal from the social ills of society, but on penetration into its structures. Social ministry and evangelism cannot be viewed as an activity, but as our way of life.

Guidelines for Adjusting the Tension

If we want to make the proper adjustment between evangelism and social ministry, we need to agree on the basic guidelines. Dr. Fenton gives four.[3]

1. Any program of social action which is part of missions must point men to, not away from, the central message of redemption through the blood of Christ.

2. Our expression of social concern must provide, whenever possible, a spoken witness to Christ.

3. We must make sure that our efforts do not arouse idealistic and unscriptural expectations. Any explanation of man's social ills which overlooks his broken relationship with God is superficial and inadequate.

4. Our desire to do good in the name of Christ should not lead us into wasteful competition with secular agencies.

A local church can begin adjusting the tension between evangelism and social ministry by assessing its own unique needs in its own setting. It is easy to recognize needs in another country, in another state and in another part of the city. But we should begin at home.

An assessment of needs can be done several ways. Members can go door-to-door and survey people living in the neighborhood. You can contact social and relief agencies who may have information about your community. Exchange concerns with other churches ministering in the area. This will help bring target groups to the surface. Awareness of target groups in the area must reach the conscious level of the church's constituency.

Once the target groups have been identified, the necessary resources to meet the needs of these people must be found. The first resource to identify is people available to help with the work. Don't attempt to launch any ministry to anyone unless you have people enlisted to do the job. Examine programs used in other churches. But remember, no program will be successful unless it meets the needs in the church's local community. Successful programs in one area may not be successful in another location. And no church can meet all the needs of all the people in its community.

Take care not to duplicate what other churches and agencies are already doing in your community. Most churches will welcome your willingness to cooperate. In one neighborhood in Portland, churches organized a people bank. If someone in the community had a plumbing problem, for instance, and was not physically or financially able to fix it, he or she could call a central number and someone with plumbing skills in the area would be assigned to do the work.

As your church moves to adjust this tension, your pastor

must preach clearly about evangelism and social ministry. No amount of policy statements and programs will take the place of faithfully proclaiming the Word of God. There needs to be a prophetic voice of the whole counsel of God. This means that the issues that Jesus addressed in the Sermon on the Mount and that the Old Testament prophets confronted must be faced in a 20th Century context.

Before a large scale program is launched, it is wise to do something on a smaller scale, such as a "pilot project." Any programs which the leaders support need to be bathed in prayer. Any ministry of your church is a ministry of everyone in the church, not only those directly involved.

Getting Involved in Your Community

Neither evangelism nor social ministry are options for either the church or for individual Christians. Both are obligations. *And obligations must precede inspiration.* We do not perform these tasks because we feel like doing them, but because we must do them. A sense of urgency accompanies God's command. It is up to your church's leaders to motivate and train your church family to reach both the communities where you work and live and also where your church is located.

An honest response to our obligation is to get involved and minister to the people in our community. It is not sufficient to throw gospel bombs and carry picket signs. And eliminating the social ills of society must not be the goal. Our goal is to change the lives as well as the circumstances of the victims. We are to make it clear to those to whom we minister that although we "hate the sin," we "love the sinner."

This applies to your church corporately and to the leaders of your church. Both are involved in adjusting the tension in this vital area. So are individual families and family members.

Not everyone will have the same concerns. Not everyone will be able to become involved in the same ministries. But everyone can get involved in his or her own neighborhood or community. If we are to truly be "World Christians," we must begin at home.

Footnotes

1. Preus, Dr. David W., *ACTS* (Minneapolis, MN: Office of Communication and Mission Support of the American Lutheran Church), p. 3.

2. Sherwood, Eliot Wirt, *The Social Conscience of the Evangelical* (NY, Evanston, and London: Harper & Row), p. 151.

3. *Ibid.*, p. 152.

8

Microphones In Front of the Trumpets

The Tension Between Contemporary and Old-Fashioned Music

"Who picks out the hymns in this church?" the young lady asked as she shook hands with me at the door, after the worship service.

"I do," I responded with a lack of confidence.

"Do you know anything about music?" she snapped back in a less than conciliatory tone.

"Well, really, I don't know too much about music; I choose the hymns for the message of the words in the hymn rather than the music."

"That's obvious," she snapped. (Actually, I didn't know anything about music. In college I had chosen art appreciation over music appreciation to meet the graduation requirement.)

She was the first person to question my hymn selections. She wasn't the last. I invited her to meet with me the next week to help me understand more about the kind of hymns that were appropriate for Sunday services. She explained that every hymn we had sung that morning was in 6/8 time. They all "sounded like waltzes," she said. Since I didn't know too much about waltzes, I assumed that she meant that the hymns were slow.

I don't choose the hymns that are sung in our services anymore. The music director does. The tension regarding what music we sing in the church remains, however. In fact, during the past decade it has intensified. On the back of the registration form that we ask people to fill out each Sunday, there is a place to write a message to the pastor. One week there was a terse rhetorical question: "Did you know that the newest song we sang today was over 100 years old?" The next week another person commented as she shook hands at the door, "It sure would be nice to sing some hymns that we know, occasionally."

It is amazing how musical tastes vary in a congregation. Most families in churches have a wide variety of musical preferences within their homes. Although all of our ears are made the same, our musical tastes differ. Some people claim that the differences are merely preferential; others say that the differences are cultural; others cite philosophical differences; while others believe it is merely a generational gap.

One person said that he didn't trust anyone who was over 30 years of age. In fact, he also said he didn't trust anyone under 30 years of age. Someone asked him how old he was. "Thirty," he answered. Although the difference between preferring "old-fashioned" or "contemporary" music is usually determined along generational lines, it is not exclusively so.

We are products of our environment. If our contemporaries prefer certain kinds of music, these are the kinds we learn to enjoy. When I was growing up there was a constant struggle over the location of the dial on the car radio. We didn't own a TV, a video, a stereo, or a cassette player. My mother wanted the dial set on the Christian station all the time. I continually switched it to a station that played popular music. Her friends appreciated and enjoyed Christian music, and my friends liked the popular music of my day.

In those days, when a certain type of music was played, a certain kind of words accompanied it, and vice versa. You could immediately tell by the sound of the music what the lyrics were. That is not true anymore. Today there are gospel words which are sung to music that many Christians associate with the world's music. It is ironic that some of the tunes of the hymns we sing in church today are the same ones that were sung in taverns generations ago.

One Sunday evening we had a musical group of Christian young people singing at our church. They had sung for us on several previous occasions, and though lively, their music was quite traditional. As they set up their sound system before the service, I could see that their style of music had changed. They had changed to a contemporary sound. They placed microphones in front of the trumpets. When they began their musical package that evening, three adults over 65-years-old headed for the doors. The contemporary musical sounds drove them away.

What Is 'Contemporary'?

A tension in many churches today exists between people who desire "contemporary" music in worship and those who want "old-fashioned" songs. In churches we use the word "contemporary" to describe not only the music, but the preaching and worship styles. We use the word in two different ways. First, as a noun. "Contemporary" in this sense means "one of the same or nearly the same age as another." We also use "contemporary" as an adjective. In this sense, we mean "marked by characteristics of the present period." The latter meaning is the one to which people usually refer. It means "not traditional or old-fashioned, recent as opposed to ancient." It may simply mean modern or up-to-date.

Trying to relate this definition to music in a local church raises some significant questions. Dr. Warren Wiersbe, a teacher on the Back To The Bible Broadcast, wrote an article entitled "Contemporary or Temporary?" He asked the important question, "Contemporary to whom?" He then explained, "Most families have at least three generations living, and some have four. Is the music 'contemporary' to me, my son, or my uncle? It is my guess that contemporary music probably means contemporary to whatever kind of music is popular in the secular world at that time."[1]

When many people refer to contemporary music in the church, they are referring to much more than just the sounds. In some people's minds, contemporary relates to the appearance of the musicians, the instruments they use, the setting and the props that are used. These people have expanded the meaning of contemporary to mean the use of guitars, horns and percussion instruments, rather than the organ or piano. It may mean the use of an overhead projector with words shown on a screen rather than using a hymnal. In some cases the change adds to the effectiveness of the music presented, and at other times it is nothing more than novelty. Wiersbe comments, "Change for the sake of change is simply novelty, and it does not last. Change for the sake of improvement is progress, and progress is what we need."[2]

Everyone agrees that the church must reach the current generation for Christ. Hymns that were written a century ago were written in a style and manner contemporary to that generation. What should we do with the "old-fashioned" hymns that are in our hymn books? One response is to revise the hymns just as we have revised our translations of the Scripture. Austin C. Lovelace in the *Journal of Church Music* comments, ". . . there is a different intent behind speech and singing. New translations which make meanings clear and understandable are commendable; but hymns are for singing and the poetry is designed to emphasize feelings and emotions as well as meanings. A good poet is sensitive to sounds, rhythms, flow, cadences and poetic devices which lead to evocative language. If the meaning is wrong in the hymn it should not be sung, but altering most hymn texts does little to change the original thought of the poet to a better understanding, and it does create confusion and anger in singers who know the hymns."[3]

Revisions are made for a variety of reasons — sexist language, military references, theological errors, outdated expressions and the use of too many personal pronouns. I would agree with Lovelace that if a hymn no longer says what we believe, we should replace it rather than revise it. A seminary professor of mine once said, "Heresy is sung in the church before it is ever preached there." The church today needs to encourage people to write or find new hymns that are meaningful to the younger generation as well as that speak to older generations.

Richard Allen Bodey, a professor at Trinity Evangelical Divinity School, asks some very meaningful questions of the older generation of people in our churches. "Why do we assume that the Holy Spirit has canonized our traditional rhythms, beats and meters? Why do we imagine that God winces when someone accompanies the songs of His people on a guitar, instead of a four or five manual organ? Where did we get the notion that our music is more sanctified if we freeze it in 18th and 19th century molds?"[4] Some people, however, prefer Bach not because of generational or philosophical difference, but simply as a musical preference.

Is there a difference between identifying with the world as part of a culture, or identifying by imitating the habits and tastes of the world? In other words, in our attempts to relate to heathen tribes would we dress like a witch doctor and use Christian words to rhythmic drum beats? Probably not. Music, however, often addresses the soul of a people through their culture and nationality. For example, "Finlandia" and "Eidel-weiss," even when adapted to Christian lyrics, may evoke nationalistic sentiments.

Is it Moral? Immoral? Amoral?

Is there such a thing in music as guilt by association? Richard Dinwiddie, a church music conference speaker writing in *Christianity Today* comments, "Many contemporary Christian artists strive to imitate certain secular artists. Dress, physical mannerisms, vocal style and even manner of presentation, are carefully contrived to create as close a similarity as possible to the image of the popular model. Some arduously seek the approval of the secular music world."[5] Amy Grant, for instance, changed her style from "mellow to lively pop rock with lots of synthesizer" to appeal to the secular market.[6]

I cannot settle the question of guilt by association in this chapter, but it is an important issue. One mid-1980s Christian group called "Stryper" (which takes its name from Isaiah 53:5, "with His stripes we are healed"), was described in *Time Magazine* this way: "the four young men on the stage . . . in their tight leather and spandex costumes crisscrossed with garish black and yellow stripes, piles of makeup, spiky hair and enough dangling chains to tie up half the elephants in Africa. . . . Instead of throwing drumsticks into the audience, these metal missionaries toss about 500 imitation leather copies of the New Testament. Stryper is only one of dozens of groups preaching the timeless message in new ways."[7]

Music that is "old-fashioned" is no longer the only music that is associated with Christianity. One of the fastest growing trends in the music industry is "Contemporary Christian." Some people see music basically as a means of expression and rock music as the music of this generation. Steve Taylor, who writes and performs his own songs, puts it this way, "Rock is associated with evil, but that is guilt by association. Music is music, and it is the vehicle of expression for my generation."[8]

Is music just music? Is the medium the message? Are the associations in certain types of music or performance so strong that the message becomes fuzzy or at best weak? People over 45 usually either don't listen to the words of contemporary Christian music or can't hear the words because the music is foreign to their generation. On the other hand, teenagers have difficulty listening to the words of traditional hymns sung in churches because the music is foreign to them.

Is music moral, immoral, or amoral? Many Christians believe it is not amoral, but either moral or immoral. Can Christian words be used with any popular secular music to effectively present the gospel to the unsaved? Are lyrics the only thing that matters? According to Chuck Smith, pastor of Calvary Chapel in Southern California, "As far as Christian music goes, it should only be used to attract people to the message. Music has no real spiritual value in and of itself. All it can do is attract people to hear the message. To me, the lyric content has always been primary.... It's the message that has validity, not the music."[9]

Is the message the same even when the performers are different, the instruments are different, the music is different, or the style is changed? These questions will be explored by musicologists. The church's primary concern is to focus on music played in the church, and especially the music used in worship of our Lord—not music played outside of the church.

How Music Fits into Worship

What is worship? Agreeing on the purpose of worship and on how music relates to worship will help us to face questions about the type of music that is appropriate for our corporate worship experience. Worship, according to *Webster's Dictionary*, is "The reverent love and affection accorded Deity." The term "worship" comes from an Anglo-Saxon word which means "worthship."

According to Allen & Borror, authors of the book *Worship: Rediscovering the Missing Jewel*, Worship is an active response to God whereby we declare His worth. Worship is not passive, but participative. Worship is not simply a mood, it is a response. Worship is not just a feeling, it is a declaration."[10]

Today there is a danger of music in the church shifting from an emphasis on the experience of worshiping God to a focus on musicians who are trying to entertain the people. Soren Kierkegaard used the analogy of a drama to explain the involvement of a congregation in worship. Usually we picture those who are on the platform as the entertainers or actors. We view God as the director or the producer who is offstage giving the cues to the performers. We view the congregation — ourselves — as the spectators. Kierkegaard said that the proper focus is that the people in our congregation are the actors, those who are "up front" are to help lead the worship, and that God is the audience. Richard Allen Bodey comments, "While music contributes significantly to the spiritual experience of the worshipping congregation, its human value and effect are of secondary importance. All music in our services of worship should be, first and foremost, a sacred offering, a holy sacrifice in song to Almighty God."[11]

Watching athletic events and TV programs has made us a nation of spectators. Worship demands personal involvement. Although most members of a congregation are not educationally equipped to understand the importance of music in worship, all believers are equipped spiritually. Singing to God is an expression of the heart, not a form of art. Every Christian has the responsibility to sing unto the Lord.

Passages in Ephesians 5:18 and Colossians 3:16 clearly describe a believer's responsibility in worship. Ephesians 5:18 states, "Do not get drunk on wine, which leads to debauchery. Instead, be filled with the Spirit. Speak to one another with psalms, hymns and spiritual songs. Sing and make music in your heart to the Lord, always giving thanks to God the Father for everything, in the name of our Lord Jesus Christ." Colossians 3:16 says, "Let the word of Christ dwell in you richly as you teach and admonish one another with all wisdom, and as you sing psalms, hymns and spiritual songs with gratitude in your hearts to God."

There are several basic teachings about worship in these passages. First, worship must be biblically based. Our expression of worship must be based on the Word of God. Second, our understanding of worship must be theocentric — centered on God. The object of worship is not the composer, or the musician, or the music, or the instruments. Some people feel that when we applaud after someone has sung, we have reverted to an actor/audience mindset. Our worship and our music must be for the glory of God. Both Ephesians 5:18 and Colossians 3:16 indicate that the focus of worship is the work of Jesus Christ.

Third, the passages indicate that music is an expression of the heart. The melody that comes from our lips must arise from an experience of the heart. Another important teaching in this passage indicates that as we praise the Lord together, Christians will be edified. The basic purpose of music is not to reach the lost, although it does prepare hearts for the Lord's message which comes through the preaching of the Word. Finally, we need to come prepared to enter His gates with thanksgiving in our hearts.

The basic content of worship is fixed, but how that is expressed will vary. Robert E. Webber in his book *Worship Old and New* comments that, "Many variables of worship are determined by cultural context. How one sits, what kind of music is played, and whether the service is spontaneous or highly formal are of secondary importance. Therefore, though worship always expresses the fixed content, it will vary from place to place."[12]

As a pastor, I was certainly grateful for the wonderful music that I learned from the hymn book. In fact, outside of the Bible, hymnals are the most important books I own. God has used the great hymns of the faith to help me grow personally and to minister to others in a variety of ways.

As a pastor, I was also grateful for the many positive additions that younger generations have brought to our worship experience. In many ways contemporary music and ideas have enriched our services. Many newer hymns and choruses are beautiful expressions of God's love. The Scriptural choruses of today are a tremendous improvement over many of the meaningless choruses we sang as I was growing up in church, for example, "It's Bubbling," "Do Lord," "Gospel Train," "Give Me Oil In My Lamp," "Climb Up Sunshine Mountain," etc. Using musical instruments such as guitars, using overheads and repetition, and singing a number of songs consecutively all have added to involvement in worship.

Does a church need to decide to use either "old-fashioned" or "contemporary" music? Is it possible to use both kinds? Is the tension between the two types of music going to become divisive or enriching? I believe that all generations can learn from each other so that our corporate worship experience is enriched.

If music is to have an important place in the church, people of all ages must be involved. A way to begin is to help people understand what part music is to play in the worship service in your church. An elective course on Worship and Music can be offered for adult Sunday school. Seminars for children on music can be planned by a music director or a music committee within the church or among several churches.

How to Increase Music Appreciation

The basic guidelines for using music in the Sunday morning worship service apply to other services as well. Here are several pointers which will help to ease the tension and to create a greater appreciation for music in worship. As you read, evaluate your own attitudes about these guidelines.

1. *Agree on the Priority of Worship.* For many years the main objective of many churches has been evangelism. Some also include edification as an important objective. They may list these two as "reaching out" and "reaching in." In the last few years some churches have added a third objective, "reaching up." This is the objective of worship. Although worship has been regarded as important, in many churches it only recently has become an objective. Worship is to be a part of the Sunday experience, and a priority in the total program of the church.

2. *Agree on the Purpose of Music.* Worship must be directed to God. Some of the music today is on a horizontal level, focusing on human relationships. Worship through music must ascribe glory to God, just as should everything else that we do (1 Cor. 10:31). In music our emphasis is praise and adoration rather than meeting needs and stirring emotions.

3. *Agree on Participation in Music.* Music is something given to all believers. In congregational worship, music is to be a corporate experience. No member of the body, no matter how poor his or her voice, should be excluded. Those who lead in worship are to give time and effort to ensure meaningful involvement of the entire congregation in music.

4. *Agree on the Message of the Music.* The words that are sung are to be biblically based and Christ-centered. The focus of singing should relate to the great transactions of God with Man—Creation, Incarnation, Crucifixion, Resurrection, Regeneration and the Second Coming. The message of Christ is not to be diluted or deleted.

Words must be clearly understood. If people can not understand the words, or the words have a double meaning, it will detract from their worship experience. Whether people use a hymn book or an overhead projector, they need to clearly see and understand the words.

5. *Agree on the Spiritual Qualifications of the Musicians.* Those who are involved in the music ministry of a church should exhibit the fruits of the Spirit just as much as those who preach and teach. We should not consider musicians to be entertainers or performers, but men and women leading in worship and praise. Bill Gothard comments, "It would be more logical and less dangerous to let an unskilled doctor operate on your heart than an unspiritual musician to minister to your soul."[13] Richard Allen Bodey adds, "There is no room at the organ console or in the choir loft of the Christian church for anyone who is not a believer. A person may have outstanding musical abilities and talents. He may have received extensive professional training. . . . But unless he is trusting Jesus Christ as his Savior and is living under His sovereign Lordship, he has no rightful place in the ministry of sacred music. None at all."[14]

6. *Agree on the Quality of the Music.* When I was a pastor in a church in rural Michigan, several times a year we had "Home Talent Night" on Sunday evening. Anyone who wanted to play or sing anything could do it. We had every instrument from musical saws to harmonicas. The emphasis was definitely on "home" and not on "talent." Many times since then I have felt that the music which preceded my preaching was a comedy of errors and I was the last act. ". . . Away with everything tawdry, cheap and vulgar! Away with frivolous tunes that give no higher purpose than to set our feet to tapping! Away with frothy, sentimental ditties that do nothing more than provide us with short-lived emotional kicks! . . . In our sacrifice of song, as in everything else, let us offer God nothing but our best."[15]

Both the music and musicians should be selected and screened.

Our worship service should never be an Amateur Hour. Thank God for the many dedicated and talented musicians who use their gifts and talents in the local church.

7. *Agree on the Need for Variety of Music.* Because there are different ages and different musical tastes in your congregation, it would be good to expose the people in your church to a variety of music, as long as that music glorifies God. The younger generation needs to appreciate the heritage of hymns preferred by the older generation. The older generation needs to develop an ear for new kinds of music that minister to the younger generation. Differences need not be divisive, but can be seen as opportunities to enrich the ministry of music in the life of the church.

As we are sensitive to the needs of the entire congregation, and trust the guidance of the Holy Spirit, the music ministry of the local church can be an exciting venture. The tension between contemporary and old-fashioned music can be adjusted so that a proper balance is maintained.

Footnotes
1. Wiersbe, Warren W., "Contemporary or Temporary?," Back To the Bible Broadcast, Lincoln, NE.
2. *Ibid.*
3. Lovelace, Austin C., "Hymn Tinkering — Gnats or Camels?," *Journal of Church Music*, Nov. 1985, Fortress Press, Philadelphia, PA, pp. 7-9.
4. Bodey, Richard Allen, "The Sacrifice of Song," *Voices*, Vol. XI, No. 3, 1985, Trinity Evangelical School, Deerfield, IL, pp.3-5.

5.   Dinwiddie, Richard D., "Moneychangers In the Church; Making the Sounds of Music," *Christianity Today*, June 26, 1981, p. 17.

6.   "The Packaging of Amy Grant," *His*, December 1985, p. 17.

7.   *TIME*, March 11, 1985, p. 60.

8.   *Ibid.*

9.   Collins, John, "A New Wave In Christian Music," Harvest, Summer 1985, p. 35.

10.   Allan, Ronald and Borror, Gordon, *Worship: Rediscovering the Missing Jewel* (Portland, OR: Multnomah Press, 1982), p. 16.

11.   Richard Allen Bodey, *op. cit.*

12.   Webber, Robert E., *Worship Old and New* (Grand Rapids, MI: Zondervan, 1982), p. 198.

13.   "Basic Principles of Music", Institute of Basic Youth Conflicts, Oak Brook, IL, 1985.

14.   Richard Allen Bodey, *op. cit.*

15.   *Ibid.*

9

The Service Never Began — It Exploded

The Tension Between Structure and Spontaneity

The church service was to begin at 6:00 p.m. Although Anita and I had attended many kinds of church services over the years, this situation was different. We were in the deep South. Our relatives had asked us to attend the evening service with them. It was a rural location, the people were blacks and the group was pentecostal.

When we arrived, only the pastor — who was called "bishop" — and his family were there. He greeted us and ushered me to a seat of honor behind the pulpit. There I sat by myself for about 15 minutes, until the service began.

They used no bulletin and no preplanned order of service. Nobody led. Nobody gave a call to worship or prayed the invocation. The worship service never began — it exploded! People suddenly started singing, accompanied by loud piano playing and tamborines.

They praised God. Everybody, children and adults, was totally involved. There was shouting, dancing and clapping.

Then it came time for testimonies. Most of the 25 people there gave a testimony. I tried to enter into the spirit of the evening, but didn't know any of the tunes. Also, I felt conspicuous because I had trouble clapping in rhythm. (A black pastor friend of mine said that after he had visited several white churches, he could clap on beat or off beat.)

After about an hour and a half of singing and testifying, it was time for the pastor to preach. By this time the atmosphere was really charged and the people were on the edge of their seats. The pastor got up and welcomed me to their church and then proceeded to tell the people that I was going to preach the sermon. I almost died on the spot. No one had even asked. In my thirty years of preaching I had never found myself in this predicament.

The previous week's sermon notes were in my Bible, but there was no way I could use them. I had preached that sermon to an educated white Baptist congregation in urban Portland, Oregon. All I could do was breathe a short prayer and ask the Holy Spirit to give me the words to say. And He did!

I preached for about 35 minutes. The presence and power of the Holy Spirit were evident as I preached with conviction and freedom. The next day I could not remember a word I had said.

Later, as Anita and I wondered why the pastor hadn't asked me beforehand, we thought we discovered the reason. The pastor was bi-vocational. He worked 40 hours a week in a large city a couple of hours away from his home. On the weekend he'd drive to the rural area where he lives. On Saturday and Sunday he'd preach two or three times and conduct an hour-long radio broadcast. He had neither the time nor adequate resources for sermon preparation. When he preached he relied completely on the Holy Spirit to give him the message.

In his mind, an educated Baptist preacher from Portland with a seminary education and four degrees shouldn't need any advance notice before he preaches. The man had no way of knowing that I spend a good portion of every week in sermon preparation. He didn't know that I decide what I'm going to preach a year in advance.

A Tension in Many Churches

This story illustrates a tension in many churches between structure and spontaneity. But the tension isn't limited to the area of preaching. It cuts much deeper. Under the surface, the tension is often based upon people's totally divergent philosophies and approaches. The trend in society today seems to be against anything that smacks of conformity, convention, rules, regimentation and ceremony. All of these words are part of what many people call structure. Spontaneity, on the other hand, we typify with words such as alive, fresh, exciting, warm, or uninhibited.

"Letting your hair down," "gut-level reaction," "hang loose," and "do it" are expressions that describe many people's approach to life. If we carried their thinking into the church we would say that if any people need to be spontaneous, it ought to be Christians. People who want spontaneity in the church claim that structure stifles creativity, hampers relationships and hinders progress.

Those who support structure in the church, on the other hand, claim that spontaneity produces confusion, shallowness and lack of stability. They believe that not much that is excellent or lasting can result from spontaneity.

Although people who tend to line up on the side of structure are older, while those who support spontaneity are usually younger, there are other factors that influence a person's preference. Geography, culture, education and occupation all have a bearing on how we view the tension between spontaneity and structure. This tension permeates every area of the church. But it seems to come into sharpest focus in three primary areas of church life: organization, worship services and relationships.

Organization Of The Church

In Acts 2:42, we see that the early church members devoted themselves to the apostles' teaching, to fellowship, to breaking bread and to prayer. There appeared to be very little, if any, discernible structure. In the succeeding chapters we see the church become more organized as it searches for the best ways to face problems and perform its ministry. The purpose of structure was not to stifle ministry, but to facilitate it. Form seemed to follow function.

As the church grew, bureaucracy developed. People lost sight of the purpose. Over the centuries, leaders became managers instead of servants, and entrepreneurs instead of shepherds. Christian organizations began to take their direction from businesses. Layers of organizations in pyramid fashion became task-oriented rather than people-oriented.

It appears that the genuine freedom which the early church experienced has become styled by buildings, constitutions, membership, church boards, trustees, clerks and business meetings. Anyone who tries to begin a new church struggles with how much structure is essential.

Years ago, when I was the founding pastor of a new church, we invited a group of churches in our area to form a Recognition Council. The purpose of the council was to examine our history, membership and organization to see if we could become formally accepted as a Baptist church. Everything went smoothly until one of the council members asked, "Where do you find trustees in the Bible?" Not only was I unable to answe his question, I even wondered if the concept of trustees was biblical. Another member of the council got me off the hook. He replied, "Trustees are found in the same verse where you find the clerk and the treasurer."

Sometimes there seems to be little connection between the First Century church and the church today. Agendas, plans, goals and committee meetings seem to be totally unrelated to the operations of the First Century church.

When I tried starting a church in a new community in Southern California, I couldn't figure out why the number of attenders wouldn't grow. We had five sharp young couples who loved the Lord. We had great times studying the Scripture in weekly Bible studies. But nobody seemed to be interested in taking any responsibility. Every time I suggested that we needed to get organized, the subject changed. Most of these people had been burned out from overinvolvement in the churches where they had previously attended. After I was no longer associated with the group, I discovered that some of them had been associated with a movement called "Acts 29." They wanted nothing to do with structure and organization. All they wanted was to keep having prayer and Bible study. Several years later I heard that the movement had died. The reason for its demise was, you've guessed it, lack of organization.

Most of us can identify with how these people felt. Many churches are overorganized. In fact, some churches even have a committee on committees. One pastor lamented that before he could hang a picture of his family on the wall of his office, he had to check with five committees. This is why many leaders jokingly complain that they are "committeed unto the Lord!"

People who oppose structure in a church accuse those who favor it of being more concerned with the task than with people. Many people don't want managers and leaders. They want coordinators and facilitators. If the church is a body, it can't function like an organization, but must function like an organism. Jesus Christ is the Head of this organism.

Those who favor a church that is structured point to the fact that Christian organizations are different from other organizations. A Christian organization is one that gives God the glory under the Lordship of Christ. Tools such as management by objectives, goals, budgets, constitutions, committees, long-range plans and agendas are used to help accomplish the purpose. Authority, control and evaluation only become necessary to ensure that the purpose is accomplished. Before discussing how this tension can be adjusted in your church, let us focus in on another part of tension.

Services Of The Church

There is probably no place in the church where the tension between structure and spontaneity is more apparent than during the time of corporate worship. Some churches have an order of service that covers two pages in the bulletin, and doesn't seem to change from week to week. In other churches it is apparent from the outset that there has been no advance planning.

In a structured worship service everything is predictable. Although most people could not name the elements of their service, they can tell you if one thing is out of place. Some people see this structure as synonymous with deadness. Churches like this are referred to as the "First Church of the Deep Freeze, where many are thawed and a few are frozen." But it's equally possible to have a dead church that is completely spontaneous.

The tension between structure and spontaneity is exemplified even before a church's worship service begins. Churches that are more structured usually prefer a time of quiet reflection and meditation prior to the service. One pastor told our church staff that he could always tell if his church was going to have a good worship service that morning by how much buzzing and noise the people made before the service. When there was plenty of activity in the congregation, it was going to be a good service.

A structured service usually begins promptly at the scheduled time with an invocation or call to worship. A spontaneous service doesn't begin, it explodes, usually with singing. If the spontaneous service begins at a scheduled time, it is usually purely by coincidence.

The two types of service are quite different. A structured service proceeds as scheduled. Usually, there is singing and Scripture reading from the hymn book. Certain acts of corporate worship may be performed each week: singing of the Gloria or the Doxology, a pastoral prayer, reading the Lord's Prayer or the Apostle's Creed, passing the offering plates, followed by a sermon. Most of the spontaneous services consist of singing of choruses, group prayer, a praise time and a message. There is much more freedom to be creative.

Because there is no way to control a spontaneous service, quitting time is of no importance. A structured service usually is monitored by the clock. Not only is the time when the service begins and ends important, but each part of the entire service as well. One pastor cautioned a group of leaders with these words, "Never give a microphone to a soprano." Unless the person who is in charge controls the microphone, it's difficult to prevent some type of spontaneity, which would throw the entire schedule off track.

One Sunday I arrived at the evening service with no message. Although I have many sermons I could have preached, none seemed appropriate. During the service that night, a woman gave a marvelous testimony of how God had been at work in her life. There was no question that the spontaneous service was what God wanted that evening.

Structure provides a sense of decency and order. The service is under control. It is shaped by people who have been placed in a position to lead. For example, on several occasions someone has come to the front of our church and said that God had urged him or her to speak to the congregation. Almost without exception I have not allowed him to speak, because God had placed me in a position of leading the service and had not spoken to me about that person's message. In a service characterized by spontaneity, a person who wanted to speak would probably be allowed to do so.

Back when I was dean of students at a seminary on the East Coast, many of our students were from the counterculture. They rebelled against the structures and formalism of churches they had known. At that time Dr. Ray Stedman had just published an excellent book called *Body Life.* It was a good corrective to the super-organization of some churches. Students wanted to use this format at the seminary chapel service. I began to notice before long that what they meant when they said they wanted a "body life" service meant being ill-prepared. No one did anything in advance. Everything was left up to spontaneity. If someone wanted to sing, he sang. If someone wanted to speak, he spoke. If people wanted to pray, they prayed. In fact, they didn't even want a leader, merely a convener.

Although this type of spontaneity was at times refreshing, it began to show the results of lack of planning. The lack of continuity and preparation detracted from the worship experience. Lack of creativity and needless duplication lowered our sense of confidence as we worshiped.

Relationships Within The Church

A friend of mine, who has worked with young people from

the counterculture for many years, once commented, "When one of these kids becomes a Christian, I try to keep him away from older Christians as long as possible." What he meant was that kids who have been under bondage in the world (alcohol, sex and drugs) needed to be set free. When these new Christians entered many churches they were introduced to a new kind of bondage. This bondage was called structured and artificial relationships.

People in churches talked differently, dressed differently, acted differently. The climate in a church was formal and unnatural. To these new Christians it seemed that people lacked honesty and were not transparent. Relationships seemed to be cold and very formal. The young people were not used to the various positions, titles, codes and ceremony in most churches. If they wanted to clap and shout, they wanted the freedom to do it. If they wanted to hug and kiss someone, they wanted the freedom to do it.

Any style of dress was appropriate. Jeans and shorts were as acceptable as a shirt and tie or a dress. People were supposed to be on a first name basis. Even if the older people referred to their pastor as Mr. or Dr., people who wanted spontaneity began breaking down the distinctions. It was difficult for some young people to discriminate between a funeral service and a "rap session," and to distinguish between the sanctuary and the gym. People who talked about long-range plans for the next ten years were talking a different language.

Those people who came from a more traditional, structured background became uncomfortable with the breaking down of structured relationships. I was one of these. My background is Prussian. We don't open ourselves up to everybody. In fact, our motto was, "I'm going to find out everything I can about you, but I don't want you to find out anything about me." As a family we were not very affectionate. Our customary greeting was a handshake. There were no hugs or kisses.

Many people were turned off by Christians who desired to be more affectionate, demonstrative and open in their relationships. We resisted sessions where you shared deep problems with complete strangers.

The tension between structure and spontaneity hits closest to home in our relationships, more so than in church organization and services. Let's look a bit deeper into this aspect of the tension.

What *Is* a Christian Relationship?

Christian relationships? Are they to be different than those we have with non-Christians? Are relationships among churches to be more spontaneous or more structured? It is not an easy tension to balance. Cultures, customs and classes differ greatly, not only from country to country, but from church to church. As we seek to adjust this tension in particular churches, we need to begin with a scriptural basis.

What does it mean in John 8:32 when Jesus says ". . .you will know the truth, and the truth will set you free"? And again in John 8:36, "So if the Son sets you free, you will be free indeed"? Although we are free from the dominion of sin, Satan, death and hell, we are not free to do as we please. We are free from the law of sin and death, but now we are alive unto Christ. Our freedom now is to serve Christ.

Is our freedom on earth different from the freedom that God's other creatures enjoy? Do we need any structures at all if we are really free in Christ? Dr. Tom Howard, former professor at Gordon College, makes a good case for our need for structure in relationships, based on God's order of creation. In the order of creation man is between the angels and animals. Both beasts and angels are completely spontaneous. Mankind is neither completely carnal nor completely spiritual, but both. Dr. Howard explains, "The first thing that we find is that we are not angels nor are we beasts, and to veer off either way is to fall into fatal error. To deny our human flesh and to be merely angelical or spiritual is to be gnostic. This is heresy, according to Christianity. On the other hand, to deny our spiritual nature and to insist with Skinner and *Playboy* that we are nothing but chemical complexes and responses, is to become precisely beastial. It seems to me that ceremony, and let me include all ritual and conventions and customs in this one word, is one of the particular and crucial ways in which we as human beings keep alive our particular nature.

"We don't, of course, know how the angels, our neighbors immediately above us do it, but we suspect that they enjoy a genuine spontaneity, where the wish and the act are one thing and where there is no breakdown in what they are designed to be. We mortal men on the other hand, are becoming what we are designed to be. We have to work at it. On the other hand, we do know how our neighbors immediately below us, the animals, do it. They enjoy genuine spontaneity as well. It is entirely in harmony with their nature because as far as we know, they too are what they are supposed to be. They do not have to curb their appetites and relationships in the name of some ulterior order that judges them."[1]

The only two times that mankind enjoyed or will enjoy complete spontaneity are in the sinless existence of the Garden of Eden and in the sinless existence that believers will find in heaven. As long as we are here on this earth, we will need some type of structure if we want to be free. Just as trains have no freedom when they leave the tracks and fish have no freedom when they leave the water, man has no freedom apart from structure.

But Christians are not trains or fish. What then is the biblical approach that will help us to adjust this tension between structure and spontaneity in our Christian relationships?

The Way of Christian Liberty

There is a difference between the way the world approaches life and the way that the children of God are supposed to live. The key concept which allows the Christian to live a different life is liberty or freedom. Liberty is the opposite of forced subjection. In the Old Testament, freedom basically referred to physical freedom. In the New Testament there are references to physical freedom, but more often it speaks about spiritual freedom.

In Galatians 5:13,14, Paul wrote, "You, my brothers, were called to be free. But do not use your freedom to indulge the sinful nature; rather, serve one another in love. The entire law is summed up in a single command: 'Love your neighbor as yourself.'" In 1 Peter 2:16, Peter equated living as a servant with true freedom, "Live as free men, but do not use your freedom as a cover-up for evil...." How is it possible to use "freedom as a cover-up for evil"?

There are two ways to use liberty wrongly. The first is called license; the other is legalism. In Jude 4 we read that there are people "who change the grace of our God into a *license* for immorality and deny Jesus Christ our only Sovereign and Lord." Obviously, there were some people who felt that salvation by grace gave them the privilege to do as they pleased, because the more they sinned, the more God had the opportunity to forgive. In Romans 6:1,2, the Apostle Paul spoke out strongly against this view. "What shall we say, then? Shall we go on sinning so that grace may increase? By no means! We died to sin; how can we live in it any longer?"

On the other hand, people also can turn liberty into legalism. Warren W. Wiersbe in his commentary on Galatians said, "We are prone to go to extremes. One believer interprets liberty as license and thinks he can do whatever he wants to do. Another believer, seeing the error, goes to an opposite extreme and imposes law on everybody. Somewhere between license on the one hand, and legalism on the other hand, is true Christian liberty."[2]

Liberty, which is true freedom, results from God's grace. It is not rules, regulations and structures, and it is not freedom to do what you want. It is freedom to serve. Structure pushed to its extreme is legalism. Spontaneity pushed to its extreme is not liberty, but license.

One key teaching that will help us adjust the tension between spontaneity and structure is known as the priesthood of the believer. This means that when a person becomes a Christian, he or she has the access and the freedom to go directly to Christ without any human assistance or structure. This is a foundational belief in evangelical churches. When I associate with other believers in a local church, however, a new dimension is added to this priesthood. Although I still go directly to Christ, my freedom is now limited by my relationship to others in the body. No longer can I live entirely spontaneously. I need some type of structure to control this relationship so that I will respect the freedom of others.

Although believers are priests before God, they are also responsible to follow the leaders of their church—people that God has chosen and gifted. Leaders are not simply examples to the flock, they equip and lead the members of the body. In Ephesians 4:11,12 the Apostle Paul says, "It was he who gave some to be...pastors and teachers, to prepare God's people for works of service, so that the body of Christ may be built up." People in a church do not have the choice to either follow their leaders or follow Christ. If God has appointed these leaders, then God's people must follow both.

3 Ways to Bring Health

Now that we have looked at how the tension fleshes itself out in church structure, services and relationships, let's go on to what can be done to bring health and growth. How is this tension between the extremes of structure and spontaneity adjusted in a local church?

1. *An Attitude Adjustment*
I once worked with a group of educators from a number of schools in the New England area. We had monthly meetings. The first notice I received said that dinner would be served at 6:00 p.m., preceded by an "attitude adjustment" hour. I discovered that this was a cocktail hour which the participants felt necessary before they could discuss issues and make decisions.

All Christians are called to be servants. Everyone, with no exceptions. And sometimes our attitudes need to be adjusted. In Philippians 2:5-7 we read, "Your attitude should be the same as that of Christ Jesus: Who, being in very nature God, did not consider equality with God something to be grasped, but made himself nothing, taking the very nature of a servant, being made in human likeness."

Mutual submission is to be our way of life as Christians. No one can justify "looking out for #1," "doing my own thing," or "my way is always the right way." Neither structure nor spontaneity in a local church can function correctly without mutual submission.

2. *A Local Adjustment*
Each local church has its own personality. No two are alike. The personality results from many factors — geographic, economic, education, racial, ethnic, cultural, etc. For instance, in one culture hugging a person of the opposite sex might b

a proper expression of Christian love. But in the Philippines this is not true. When I went there to preach, the missionaries admonished me not to hug any of the women.

The age of the people in a congregation is a factor as well. An older congregation must be treated differently. Older people need more structure in the organization, in the services and in relationships. Newer and younger people need more spontaneity. Everyone needs to recognize that both tradition and change are necessary.

Most people would prefer less structure in the church. Some go from one church to another looking for one that has just the right balance between structure and spontaneity. This balance is difficult if not impossible to achieve, because even members of an individual family have different tastes. Appreciate the emphasis of your own tradition and local church, while at the same time encouraging your leaders to be open to different approaches.

3. *A Continuous Adjustment*

Should the church reflect society or should it import society? All of us agree that the church is not to follow society. Richards and Hoeldtke in their book *A Theology of Church Leadership* point out, "The basic reality the Scripture presents is that the church is a living organism with Jesus Christ Himself functioning as Head. In seeing Jesus as Head, we must take seriously the notion that He is not Head emeritus. He is not the retired founder of the firm. No, God has appointed Jesus 'to be the head over everything for the church, which is his body'" (Ephesians 1:22,23).[3]

The church does not receive its directions from the business world, the academic community, behavioral psychologists, sociologists, or any other group. Our message is constant, fixed; but the methods that we use to accomplish God's purpose can and should be adjusted continually for effectiveness.

In 1 Corinthians 9:21,22 we read, "To those not having the law I became like one not having the law (though I am not free from God's law but am under Christ's law), so as to win those not having the law. To the weak I became weak, to win the weak. I have become all things to all men so that by all possible means I might save some." In our churches today we may not face the same kind of people or same kind of problems Paul faced. However, we need the same ability to continue to adjust our approach to reaching people with the gospel message.

Absence of structure ultimately brings chaos. Absence of spontaneity brings coldness and deadness. A proper adjustment between the two opposites comes as we discover how to have spontaneity within the structure. The way to begin this process is by initially checking our own attitudes. If we are convinced that our views are the only views regarding the subject of structure and spontaneity, then any other approach will be an intrusion or an enemy. A teachable and open spirit is essential. Next, the approach our church takes should reflect the needs of people who attend and people within the community that we're trying to reach. Finally, we need to be willing to be led by the Holy Spirit in the organizational structure and methods we use. Structure and spontaneity are means whereby we are able to fulfill our purpose, achieve our goals and meet our objectives.

Footnotes

1. Howard, Dr. Tom, "Contra Spontaneity," Gordon Conwell Theological Seminary, South Hamilton, MA, 1977.

2. Wiersbe, Warren W., *Be Free* (Wheaton, IL: Victor Books, 1975), p. 126.

3. Richard, Lawrence O. and Hoeldtke, Clyde, *A Theology of Church Leadership* (Grand Rapids: Zondervan 1980), p. 14.

10

We've Never Done It That Way Before

The Tension Between Tradition and Change

One Sunday, after the morning service, a man in his 80s was waiting to talk to me. He had patiently waited until I had greeted everyone else, but he was visibly upset. I barely had time to greet him when he blurted out, "Pastor, we are going to have to stop using all these different translations and versions of Scripture in our church." After venting his frustration for a few more minutes, he concluded by stating his conviction on the subject, "We are hindering the work of the Spirit."

For Frank, the man in his 80s, there was only one Bible — the King James Version. He could handle some of the changes in our church, but now we were going too far. When we changed both the Bibles and the hymn books, it was about too much for him. He believed that the King James Version of the Bible was the one true version.

Change is never easy, but when it runs smack against our convictions, it becomes even more difficult. Frank and many others of his generation have not changed churches for many decades. Temple Baptist Church is a 100-year-old Scandinavian church. Many of the families trace their roots in the church back five or six decades. Although these people have met in the same building for almost 60 years, the church has undergone constant change. Some of the changes that Frank's generation has had to face include language (from Swedish to English), pastors, single to multiple staff, types of music, diverse programs, service time changes, kind of people (Scandinavian to a multi-ethnic group), and the elimination of traditional activities.

Despite these changes, the church is rich in traditions. How can new people cope with so many unwritten traditions? Some of the new people attending Temple Baptist are men that I met at the racketball courts. Several have never been to church before and others come from churches with very different customs. In Sunday school class one of these men couldn't understand why we passed the offering envelope around so often. Then in the worship service we had two more offerings. Sometimes we clapped and other times we didn't. Sometimes we finished on time, but most of the time we didn't. Sometimes we sang old hymns and other times contemporary choruses. My friend didn't know any of the regular attenders in the church. In a short time, however, he seemed to understand what to do, and when and how to do it.

In every church, except a brand new one, there is a tension between tradition and change. Older people and those who have been in the church for several years view any change with suspicion. Those who are younger or new to the church find traditions to be frustrating and burdensome. How can both groups worship and serve together in the same church without being in constant conflict? Does each church need to choose between tradition and change? Can we have a growing, healthy congregation without going to either extreme?

Change Is a Way of Life

No area of life has escaped change. During the past couple of decades the pace of change has accelerated. Until the '60s and '70s, most changes in our country were technological in nature. As people began to accept this technological change, it became easier for us to tolerate changes in the political, social, economic and educational areas of our lives. In the Twentieth Century, change has become a way of life.

Although change is familiar, it does not come without pain. Adlai Stevenson, when campaigning for the presidency of the United States, commented that some people were so against change that "they would have to be dragged kicking and screaming into the 20th Century." The church is one organization that does not alter its traditions easily.

Historically, traditions were truths reported to be given to the church by Jesus and His apostles. They were passed from one person to another by word of mouth, but not recorded in the Bible. Christianity inherited a whole series of traditions from Judaism. These traditions became confused with the teachings of Christ. In Mark 7:5-9 we read, "So the Pharisees and teachers of the law asked Jesus, 'Why don't your disciples live according to the tradition of the elders instead of eating their food with "unclean" hands?' He replied, 'Isaiah was right when he prophesied about you hypocrites; as it is written: "These people honor me with their lips, but their hearts are far from me. They worship me in vain; their teachings are but rules taught by men." You have let go of the commands of God and are holding on to the traditions of men.' And he said to them: 'You have a fine way of setting aside the commands of God in order to observe your own traditions!' "

Peter wanted to make sure that the early believers were able to distinguish between what is merely tradition and what is inherent in the gospel. He wrote to them, "For you know that it was not with perishable things such as silver or gold that you were redeemed from the empty way of life handed down to you from your forefathers" (1 Peter 1:18).

As religious traditions increased in number and importance, it became imperative that they be written down. In the Roman Catholic Church many traditions are recorded in written form and are regarded as equal in importance to the Scripture. In most Protestant churches traditions are basically unwritten. They are not viewed as having doctrinal authority, but as having functional authority. They are "the way we do things around here." Some traditions have been established over the decades. Others are set in place by doing something the same way twice.

Many people see traditions as having no value in the life and ministry of a congregation. Traditions are wrong when they are no longer related to any purpose, are not meeting peoples' needs, and their significance is not communicated to newcomers. But traditions have value if they enrich the uniqueness of a church. They shape the life and the ministry of a congregation, giving it a sense of continuity with the past. They allow people to plan adequately for coming events. Traditions raise the expectations of people, especially youth. Youth look forward to sitting together in a sanctuary, staying up on New Year's Eve, attending Sunday night youth services and participating in the Summer Mission Team. These traditional activities provide a sense of excitement as well as a rallying point. Traditions can be a "powerful force in shaping the purpose, the role, the schedule, the priorities, and the performance of every congregation."[1] But traditions become an obstacle when they no longer are a positive force, but a focus of alienation. When we stop evaluating traditions and identify them with individual rather than corporate goals, it is time for a change.

Change is inevitable, but our reactions to change are not. Alvin Toffler in his book *Future Shock* describes the ways that people try to resist change. "They may 'block out' unwelcome reality and refuse to take in new information; they may look for a simple solution of all the world's ills in a single doctrine; they may withdraw into a cocoon of specialization; or they may turn their minds back to an earlier and less troublesome time and try to apply the solutions of the past to the problems of today."[2] All of us can identify with at least one of these ways that people resist change in a church.

The Gospel Is Unchanging — Our Methods Are Not

Before a church begins to change its traditions, leaders need to develop a doctrine of change and communicate this to the congregation. Many people who can accept change in many other areas cannot tolerate it in religion. They view change in any area of the church as an erosion of biblical and moral values. For them, change is to be resisted at all costs. Part of this attitude stems from their view of the doctrine of God. God, His Word and His Son are all immutable. Traditions regarding the ways we do things become confused with our beliefs about God. In fact, traditions sometimes take the place of our beliefs, such as Frank's insistence that we stick to the King James Bible. Dr. Grant Howard, professor of Pastoral Ministry at Western Conservative Baptist Seminary in Portland, Oregon, has outlined several scriptural doctrine statements which refer to change.[3]

1. *God Never Changes*

With God there is no past, present, or future, only an eternal now. In 1 Samuel 15:29 we read, "He who is the Glory of Israel does not lie or change his mind; for he is not a man, that he should change his mind." In Malachi 3:6 God tells His people, "I the Lord do not change."

2. *Nothing In This World Is Permanent*

Change is the only thing that is permanent. From the moment of birth we begin the process of not only growth, but death. Moses, in his eloquent prayer in Psalm 90:4-6 states this truth very clearly, "For a thousand years in your sight are like a day that has just gone by, or like a watch in the night. You sweep men away in the sleep of death; they are like the new grass of the morning — though in the morning it springs up new, by evening it is dry and withered."

3. *Change For the Sake of Variety Is Wrong*

Our purpose as individual believers and individual churches is to glorify God. Change that is not related to this purpose of improving God's reputation is a waste of time. In James 1:6-8 we find a description of a person who vacillates in what he does, ". . .he who doubts is like a wave of the sea, blown and tossed by the wind. That man should not think he will receive anything from the Lord; he is a double-minded man, unstable in all he does."

4. *There Are Some Changes the Believer Should Resist*

Believers are to be separated unto God and separated from the world. We are to resist Satan and the world system that is under his control. "You adulterous people, don't you know that friendship with the world is hatred toward God? Anyone who chooses to be a friend of the world becomes an enemy of God. . . . Resist the devil, and he will flee from you" (James 4:4,7).

5. *God's Program Involves Change*

God and His message remain the same, but the methods change. In Colossians 2:19 we read that ". . .the whole body, supported and held together by its ligaments and sinews, grows as God causes it to grow." We are exhorted to ". . .grow in the grace and knowledge of our Lord and Savior Jesus Christ." Both growth and maturity in Christ involve change. As infants become children and then adults, God desires that we change spiritually as well.

6. *Change Is Inherent in Evangelism and Edification*

God is not limited to any particular method, but He has chosen us to be ministers of reconciliation. Because people's interests and backgrounds are different, we must be sensitive to the best approach to use to reach them. Paul, in 1 Corinthians 9:22,23, demonstrates his versatility. "To the weak I became weak, to win the weak. I have become all things to all men so that by all possible means I might save some. I do all this for the sake of the gospel, that I may share in its blessings."

7. *Unity and Harmony Among Believers Take Precedence Over Change*

For over 25 years in the ministry, the one verse that has guided me against unnecessary and unbiblical change is Ephesians 4:3: "Make every effort to keep the unity of the Spirit through the bond of peace." Change, even if it is supported by the majority of the people, should be delayed until the process does not threaten to destroy the unity of the Holy Spirit in the body.

8. *A Change Could Be Wrong At One Time and Right At Another*

God's will for the church includes His perfect timing. In Ecclesiastes 3, the writer begins the chapter by saying, "There is a time for everything, and a season for every activity under heaven. . . ." Then he lists several examples of activities that may be right at one time and not right at another time. In verse 4 he says, ". . . a time to weep and a time to laugh, a time to mourn and a time to dance. . . ." In verses 6-7 he says there is a "time to search and a time to give up, a time to keep and a time to throw away, a time to tear and a time to mend, and a time to be silent and a time to speak. . . ."

9. *Some Changes Are Neither Right Nor Wrong, But Are Neutral*

Many changes result from someone's beliefs and convictions, while others are the result of opinions and preferences. We are not to condemn or judge individuals because of the choices they make in areas where God has granted us liberty. Paul gives us an example of how to handle differences between believers. In Romans 14:2,3 we read, "One man's faith allows him to eat everything, but another man, whose faith is weak, eats only vegetables. The man who eats everything must not look down on him who does not, and the man who does not eat everything must not condemn the man who does, for God has accepted him."

Creating a Climate for Change

Once we have developed a doctrine of change in the local church, we are in a better position to adjust the tension that comes with change. Areas in church life which need to be under constant review for possible change are: policies, procedures, programs, personnel and goals. Changes that are beneficial to everyone or to the vast majority are much easier to accept.

Changes that inconvenience us in any way are difficult to accept. For instance, if the church has a tradition of having a Christmas Eve service from 11:00 p.m. until Midnight, it can be stressful to change, no matter what the reason. If there are younger families, however, who are not able to come because of small children in the family, what should the church do? Any change will affect those who have traditionally celebrated Christmas Eve at an 11:00 p.m. church service. Would you continue to meet at 11:00 p.m. and thereby eliminate the younger families? Would you satisfy the younger families by having a 6:00 p.m. service? Would you have a service at 9:00 p.m. and alienate both groups? Would you have two different services — one at 11:00 p.m. and one at 6:00 p.m.? Would you alternate the times each year? Would you eliminate the entire service due to differences?

Most people in a local church will not have an active part

in making a decision about the time and nature of the Christmas Eve service. What are they to do about this tension? Each family must make its own decision. Years of family tradition cannot be and often should not be altered because of a conflict with church scheduled programs. You cannot attend everything on the church schedule. It is never God's will for us to be in two places at once. As a family, you can discuss creative ways to be involved in both family and church events. The one does not need to cancel out the other.

Most changes are resisted in one way or another. The amount of resistance depends on several factors. All change is perceived as loss and is usually painful. Why do people resist change? Roy Zuck, a professor at Dallas Theological Seminary, gives five reasons.

1. If the changes imply less security
2. If the changes imply criticism of the present situation
3. If the changes imply additional effort
4. If the changes imply personal loss
5. If the changes seem unnecessary or unhelpful[4]

Faced with the inevitable resistance to any change, leaders in a church need to create a climate for change. Before any significant lasting change can be accomplished, people must have an attitude of trust and confidence in the leadership. This does not happen overnight. Remember that "the process is as important as the product." Changes take time. People need to know that their opinions and ideas are respected. Leaders must be willing to spend time discussing new ideas and be tolerant of dissent and disagreement. We must learn to agree to disagree agreeably.

Whether or not change will be effective does not depend on the action taken, but on the approach taken by those who are in the position of authority. Leaders must see themselves as facilitators or change agents rather than as dictators who demand that people change. If a leader wants the support of people, he or she cannot be perceived as a person who uses people. A facilitator does not simply make the changes without involving anyone else, then face the repercussions after the change has taken place.

Nor does a facilitator sit back and respond to problems as they occur. A person with this leadership style looks at a crisis as an opportunity to pick up the pieces and make the best out of a bad situation. Instead, a facilitator anticipates change. His anticipatory approach to planning, according to Lyle Schaller, emphasizes knowing both the problems and potential for change and enlisting others to help him carry it out.[5]

Changes in the church should be tied to existing conditions where there is already discontent. It is easier to begin making changes when most people recognize that change is necessary. Begin with the minor changes first.

5 Ways We Respond to Change

Because change is a process, it is essential that you use proper timing when initiating change. Whatever the change is, and whenever the change occurs, people will generally fall into one of five categories in their response to the change process. Church growth expert, Win Arn, describes the categories and the percentage of people in each group.[6]

Innovators—2%. These are the idea people. People in this category are always dreaming and planning how things could be better. They are not content with the status quo. Most of the time these people are not in a position of authority or policy making in the church. Many people in this category have the spiritual gift of faith (1 Corinthians 12:8,9). Idea people don't focus on the way things are, but look at the potential. Innovators have learned to think big and are optimistic. Usually they are not hung up on whether or not they receive the credit for an idea.

Early adopters — 18%. These are people in a church who are very positive. Many in this category have the gift of wisdom. When they hear a good idea, they are not tentative in their support. Usually these people encourage the leaders to "go for it." "When are we going to get started?" they respond to the idea.

Middle Adopters — 60%. This is the majority of people, who want to be cautious. Perhaps their attitude is, "Be not the first by which the new is tried, and be not the last to lay the old aside." One of their first questions is, "Whose idea is it?" Their next question is, "Who is against it?" Basically, they find it easier to maintain the status quo than to take any risks.

Late Adopters — 18%. Quite often these are people who see their role as "putting on the brakes." People in this category often use expressions such as, "We've never done it that way before," or "We've tried that before," or "Let's not reinvent the wheel." They feel that change happens too often and too quickly to suit them. Although they will eventually go along with the majority, they will not acknowledge their support of the change, nor devote their energy to make it successful.

Laggards — 2%. This group sees any change as inherently bad. They are not only committed to the status quo, like the Late Adopters, but are tied to the past. Probably, they will never change, and quite often they become the leaders of division in the church. In one church I served, every time we voted on anything financial, there were always four negative votes. It didn't matter what people were voting for, these people felt the church shouldn't be spending money. Many of these people feel that their mission in life is to oppose anything new.

Another group in the church are one-sided for either tradition or change. Those who support tradition want to resist any kind of change. Others want to destroy all traditions and establish something new in its place. There is another group of people who want change, but not at an accelerated pace. Tradition, like change, can be both positive or negative.

In some churches change itself becomes a tradition. Every time a program or plan begins to falter, some people immediately want to change it. Change becomes a substitute for poor planning, sloppy execution and lack of perseverance. Continuity, stability and confidence demand that we keep the values that we received from good traditions.

Change in the church is necessary because its opposite is death. Those who see change as a threat to their value systems will oppose and resist anything new. Realizing that some people will resist change, leaders should not wait until everyone supports an idea. When the leaders are convinced of the benefit of a change, they need to act.

Although people have a desire to make changes successfully, it is wise not to place those who oppose the change in a winner/loser situation. Not everyone can have his own way if there are opposing views. The tension adjuster looks for ways to let each person know that his input is valued. If possible, he incorporates some of the ideas of people who don't favor the new program.

Many people who are not in leadership positions feel that there is very little they can do to accept the results of change or lack of it in their church. Change is a process. To be successful it involves collaboration. Those who aren't leaders can pray for them, make suggestions and ask questions. When decisions are made, they can show a positive attitude that supports the leaders. They can exhibit willingness to try new ideas and risk the possibility of failure.

Adjusting the Tension

If you are a leader, here are some ways that you can help adjust the tension in your church between tradition and change, in a healthy, balanced manner.

1. Anticipate change before it becomes a crisis. Leaders need to act, not always react.

2. Make sure the proposed change is based on sound scriptural principles and issues rather than on differing personalities and philosophies.

3. Gather the support of those who are in favor of the idea and will help promote it.

4. Try out the change on a smaller group such as a committee, a home Bible study group, or a Sunday school class.

5. Be flexible, do not put details into concrete.

6. Listen attentively to both those who are for and those who are against the proposed change.

7. Make sure that there will be broad ownership of the idea and an ongoing process of evaluation.

8. Before the change is finalized, give enough time to prepare and to allow for sufficient input.

9. Be willing to let other people receive the credit even if the idea was yours. Don't be concerned about who gets the credit, as long as God gets the glory.

10. Be willing to accept criticism and the possibility that the change will not be successful.

Remember, each local church is unique. It is dangerous to adopt something new from another group. What is needed and what was successful in one situation may not be the right change for another congregation. Each fellowship needs to make changes in light of its history, its constituency, its circumstances and its goals.

There is a need for wisdom to know the right time and the right way to adjust the tension between tradition and change. "If any of you lacks wisdom, he should ask God, who gives generously to all without finding fault, and it will be given to him" (James 1:5).

Footnotes

1. "The Importance of Tradition," *The Parish Paper* Vol. 11, Number 9, March 1982, Yokefellow Institute, Naperville, IL.

2. "The Royal Bank Letter," published by the Royal Bank of Canada, Vol. 63, No. 4, July/August 1982.

3. Howard, Dr. Grant, unpublished class notes, Western Conservative Baptist Seminary, Portland, Oregon.

4. Zuck, Roy B., *The Superintendent and the Dynamics of Change* (Wheaton, IL: Scripture Press Foundation: Christian Education Monographs, Superintendents Series No. 7, 1969), p. 2.

5. Schaller, Lyle, *The Change Agent* (Nashville, TN: Abingdon Press, 1972), p. 14.

6. *Growth Report*, Institute for American Church Growth, Pasadena, CA, Number 5, p. 4.

11

Rearranging the Furniture

The Tension of Setting Church Priorities

It was a hot, sticky Sunday afternoon in the early 1950s. A number of young people in my church drove into Chicago every week to teach Sunday school at the Maxwell Street YMCA. After we finished, we would wander around Maxwell Street before returning home to our Chicago suburb.

Maxwell Street was an open market where you could buy just about anything. There were all kinds of businesses operating in the neighborhood. Most were legitimate, but some were questionable. Along with the businesses, there were an assortment of characters that punctuated the local environment. Mind readers, quick change artists, magicians and street preachers made our visit each week an entertaining one.

On this particular afternoon I was walking through the market area carrying a Bible under my arm. It was so crowded that I didn't notice the shabbily dressed man who suddenly stood before me. Nobody in the crowd had ever spoken to me before, o I was startled by his direct question. Pointing to my Bible he said, "Do you believe that?" Rather hesitantly I replied, "Yes, I do." He immediately responded, "Nobody believes that! Everybody knows that Jesus was kidnapped for 18 years."

What a joke! Here was a bum from the street making such an absurd statement. I attended a Bible-believing church, had graduated from a Christian high school and had never heard anything as ridiculous as Jesus being kidnapped for 18 years. But this bum on the street's words wouldn't leave my mind.

When I got home that day, I decided to disprove his statement with Bible passages. I knew Jesus was born in a manger in Bethlehem and that He died when He was 33-years-old. As I checked further, I found that Jesus was in the Temple at age 12 and He began His public ministry at age 30. No matter how hard I searched and how many passages I read, I couldn't find anything about His life between ages 12 and 30. Eighteen years of silence! Was the bum on Maxwell Street right about Jesus being kidnapped for 18 years? Finally, I discovered one verse that spoke about that apparently silent period. Luke 2:52 describes the life of Jesus during those 18 years. "And Jesus grew in wisdom and stature, and in favor with God and men." Jesus led a balanced life. He grew intellectually "in wisdom," physically "in stature," in favor with God spiritually, and in favor with God and men socially.

But another question emerged out of my research into Jesus' life. Why did he live on this earth only 33 years? Why not 100 years, 500 years, or 969 years as Methuselah had? It seemed to me that He could have done so much more good. One day I read that the early church had reached the world during its generation. How long is a generation? According to the dictionary I consulted, "A generation is the time that it takes for the son to succeed the father, a period of time usually thought to be 33 years." Jesus had lived one generation.

You and I get two generations, more or less. Such a short time, but twice as long as Jesus had. Through research, organ transplants and better nutrition, we may get a few more years, but basically our adult life expectancy of 70 to 80 years has not changed significantly since Moses wrote Psalm 90. No matter how much money we have or how much influence we have, we are never going to get any more time than we have now. We already have all the time there is.

A Tension Between *Now* and *Then*

As a consequence, there are things that we need to do *now* and things that should be done *later*. When we wait to do things later that must be done now, and try to do things now that should wait until later, we throw our lives out of balance and into eventual turmoil.

The tension between the *now* and *then* is one that every individual continually struggles with. That tension is increased when it is compounded by corporate tension in a church.

All of us have experienced this problem of having "more things to do than we have time to do them" in our personal lives. Demands, problems and crises prevent us from doing the things that we need to do. Charles Hummel, in his excellent booklet *Tyranny of the Urgent*, states this tension very clearly. "We live in constant *tension* between the urgent and the important. The problem is that the important task rarely must be done today, or even this week. Extra hours of prayer and Bible study, a visit with that non-Christian friend, careful study of an important book: These projects can wait. But the urgent tasks call for instant action, endless demands, pressure every hour and day."[1]

Many individuals in the Scripture were guilty of violating basic principles of time priorities. Their examples of impatience — being out of step with God's timing — help us see the futility of acting hastily. In 2 Kings 5, an army commander, Naaman, had leprosy. When Elisha told him to wash seven times in the

Jordan and his skin would become clean, Naaman became angry. In verse 11, Naaman reacted to Elijah's suggestion, "I thought that he would surely come out to me and stand and call on the name of the Lord his God, wave his hand over the spot and cure me of leprosy." God wanted Naaman to learn some important lesson which he could not have learned with an instant cure.

In the New Testament, Jesus had gone to Bethany to eat with his friends Mary and Martha. This story is described in Luke 10:38-42. Mary sat at Jesus' feet while Martha was busy in the kitchen making preparations. Martha came and asked Jesus to speak to her sister about helping her with the preparations. We read that Jesus answered, "Martha, Martha, . . . you are worried and upset about many things, but one thing is needed. Mary has chosen what is better, and it will not be taken away from her."

Three Types of People in Your Church

In every church there are at least three kinds of people. The first are the *lone rangers*. They don't care what or when the church does anything. They are going to do what they want when they want to do it. Another type are the *long rangers*. Everything can wait. No sense in getting in a hurry about anything. The third group are the *short rangers*. Everything is a crisis and things must be done immediately, if not sooner.

The *lone ranger* believes he or she is under the authority of God alone, and of no other human leadership or organization. Lone rangers staunchly proclaim that they are members of the universal church, and some may even attend local churches fairly regularly. What identifies a lone ranger is not his mask of anonymity, but his independent spirit. His decision is not based on whether something in the church is to be done now or later, but whether or not it is what he wants to do. At the church's annual meeting the church adopts a budget, but the lone ranger doesn't want to support a budget — only an occasional project in which he is interested. Usually his support goes to groups and organizations outside the local church. A lone ranger feels no ownership of the goals or any corporate identity with the people of his local church.

A *long ranger*, on the other hand, is someone who doesn't want to act. Being decisive is not part of his makeup. When I was growing up there was a couple in our church who dated each other for over nine years. The basic reason that they didn't get married was that it wasn't the right time. The long ranger is usually quite tentative. It is never the right time to get married, go to school, buy a house, change jobs, or have a family.

In a church, the long ranger does not want to act on anything. The easiest thing to do is to appoint a committee. Someone has described a committee as, "put together by a group of the unwilling, who get the unable to do the unnecessary." Long rangers aren't usually willing to take risks or step out on faith. They want all the information, all the answers and all the resources in-hand before they are willing to act. By the time the long ranger is ready to act, the opportunity or the need for a decision has vanished.

In contrast, *short rangers* are usually impulsive. If they want it, they get it. If they feel they should do it, they do it. Their philosophy is usually buy now, pay later. Committees, boards, or any kind of group decision making process is seen as stifling and cumbersome. They see going through proper procedures and allowing time for discussion and study as a waste of precious time.

When we were in Japan we visited the city of Kobe, which is famous for its "beer-fed" beef. Instead of allowing beef cattle to develop and grow normally, the farmers force-feed the animals with beer. This helps the farmers to make greater prof-its in a shorter period of time. Short-rangers would think this is an excellent strategy. Our generation is using more and more instant products. It is becoming more difficult to tell or taste the difference. There are instant drinks, potatoes and cereal, as well as vegetables and fruits which are grown at accelerated rates in greenhouses. We are becoming short rangers.

Short rangers want action. Surveys, cost analyses, feasibil-ity studies and questionnaires are detours from accomplishing their objectives. The most cumbersome misdirection for them is the one called the long range planning committee. Short rangers are convinced that these are days of "ad hocism." If a committee is needed, it should be an "ad hoc" committee. "Ad hoc" means a concern for a particular end or purpose without any consideration for wider implications or applica-tions.

A church cannot achieve its objectives through lone rangers. And it cannot be successful if it eliminates either long rangers or short rangers. What works best is a healthy balance between these last two types of people. Sometimes it is essential to do things now. At other times it is better to do them later. In order to adjust the tension between the two, it is wise to distinguish between three kinds of obligations in the church: continual, seasonal and immediate.

Continual Obligations

There are some duties that we must perform continuously. These do not fall into the now or then category. One area of continuing responsibility for the church is to minister to those who are in need. In John 12, Jesus was having dinner with the family of Mary, Martha and Lazarus. During the course of the evening, Mary annointed Jesus with expensive perfume.

Judas was indignant that Jesus allowed Mary to waste something so expensive. In verse 5 he objected by saying, "Why wasn't this perfume sold and the money given to the poor? It was worth a year's wages." Jesus replied: "You will always have the poor among you, but you will not always have me" (verse 8).

Jesus' comment refers back to a continuous obligation which God commanded in Deuteronomy 15:10,11. "Give generously . . . without a grudging heart; then because of this the Lord your God will bless you in all your work and in everything you put your hand to. There will always be poor people in the land. Therefore I command you to be openhanded toward your brothers and toward the poor and needy in your land." Churches are to respond to the needy, especially within their own congregation but also within their own community. We are to extend special concern to widows and orphans (James 1:17). We cannot give this responsibility to other churches and other community agencies.

Today there are many jobless, helpless and homeless people who need our help. If a church finds itself located in an affluent community, it should offer assistance to churches located in needy areas.

Another perpetual obligation the church has is that of proclaiming the gospel. 1 Peter 3:15 clearly emphasizes the necessity of being always prepared: ". . . always be prepared to give an answer to everyone who asks you to give the reason for the hope that you have." Every member of the church is to be a continuous witness. Before Jesus Christ ascended to heaven, the apostles questioned Him about the timing of future events. Jesus answered them in Acts 1:7,8, when He said, "It is not for you to know the times or dates the Father has set by His own authority. But you will receive power when the Holy Spirit comes on you; and you will be my witnesses in Jerusalem, and in all Judea and Samaria, and to the ends of the earth."

Although we have times of special evangelistic effort and

emphases, worldwide evangelism is the continual responsibility of the church. All groups within the church should have evangelizing the lost as one of their objectives. The leaders of your church should encourage this both by example and proclamation.

Much of the tension over the nature and the urgency of worldwide evangelistic efforts is related to a church's emphasis on the Second Coming. Churches that believe in the literal return of Jesus Christ and a place called heaven and a place called hell have a different perspective on time than those who do not. When I was growing up in the 1940s, I can remember a man who stood out on the sidewalk after church distributing tracts entitled "Five Minutes to Twelve." He believed the time of Christ's return was imminent. Since that time, other people have moved the time on the prophetic clock up to 2 or 3 minutes to twelve. As we saw in Acts 1:6-8, Jesus wanted his disciples to concentrate on proclaiming the gospel, not on predictions of His return.

Any belief in the imminent return of Jesus Christ should not lead us to overemphasize the rapture of the church or the Second Advent. On the other hand, if we believe that the church is going through the tribulation, we should be witnessing rather than looking forward to survival. There are books and manuals that urge Christians to gather guns, gold and grain to prepare themselves for the coming world famine and tribulation. This overemphasis on survival is just as devastating to the Christians' witness as the emphasis of those who spend all their time and efforts waiting for the Second Coming.

What a local church believes about those who have never heard the gospel has an impact on its urgency of evangelism. Many people believe that people who have never heard the gospel will go to heaven. Let's suppose that there are 100 people on an isolated island in the South Pacific. None of these people have ever heard about Jesus Christ. If people go to heaven who have never heard about Jesus Christ, then 100% of these islanders will eventually be saved. What would happen if a missionary went to that island and was able to share the message of the gospel with all 100 of the people and over a period of time 50 people accepted Christ, but 50 people rejected Christ? Now how many would go to heaven? Only 50 percent. The inhabitants of the island would be better off if they had never heard. If the number going to hell increases after hearing the gospel, we should hire gun boats and surround the island in order to keep all missionaries away.

The Great Commission is still valid. It has never been rescinded or altered. Worldwide outreach through world Christians is still our mandate. This message "...is from God, who reconciled us to himself through Christ and gave us the ministry of reconciliation: that God was reconciling the world to himself in Christ...and he has committed to us the message of reconciliation" (2 Corinthians 5:18,19). One lady no longer attends our church because she believes that sending out missionaries is both ineffective and inefficient. She believes that the way to reach the world for Christ is through satellites. Satellites transmitting signals are no more going to reach a lost world for Christ than are gospel blimps dropping leaflets in our neighborhoods. The discipling process is done through Christians, not machines.

Seasonal Obligations

We are not to be seasonal Christians. As Christians, our message and manner of living demand that we be consistent. Paul exhorts Timothy in 2 Timothy 4:2, "Preach the Word; be prepared in season and out of season; correct, rebuke and encourage — with great patience and careful instruction." Our ministry is to be marked by faithfulness.

However, there are different seasons in the lives of individual Christians and also in the life of the local church. This presents a dilemma, in many cases a crisis. For instance, if all Christians have the continual obligation to minister to the poor and needy and also to evangelize the world, how do they justify taking time out for formal education?

Several years ago one of the young men in our church was having a hard time deciding whether to go to seminary for three years or to join the staff of an aggressive evangelistic student group. He consulted the leader of the student organization and asked whether or not he should attend seminary. The leader's reply was typical of those who fail to see the overall picture: "Going to seminary is like rearranging furniture in a burning building." In other words, "Jesus is coming, people are going to hell. Don't waste your time going to school; Jesus may come before you finish."

Jesus spent 30 years preparing for three years of ministry. The apostle Paul did not immediately jump into ministry after his conversion, but spent three years in Arabia before he went to Jerusalem (Galatians 1:15-18). There are periods in life when preparation not only is wise, but essential. Many a public personality who has had a conversion experience has immediately launched into a public ministry with no biblical training or theological base. Structured or formal training does not eliminate one's ministry for a period of his life. On the contrary, education should not be viewed as preparation *for* ministry, but preparation *in* ministry.

We live in a day when people are interested in shortcuts. Products and foods are instantly prepared. But there is no shortcut to a good education.

A seasonal obligation for most churches is a building program. Some churches are constantly involved in building construction, but for most the experience is limited to once or twice in a lifetime (although most churches spend the rest of the years paying for the building).

When the need for constructing a building becomes apparent to church leaders, the congregation usually divides itself into three groups. Some people see constructing any church building as either unbiblical or a waste of money. They state their belief that the needs of the world are so great that we can't justify such large expenditures. Buildings, for these people, become "edifice complexes," which are worshiped by those who emphasize places instead of people.

Another group wants to build, and they want to build right now. Sometimes their reasons are the same as those of people who don't want to build. They believe that Christ's return is imminent. They want to use every means at their disposal, including larger and better facilities, in order to reach more people for Christ. In their determination to get the building done now, they may look at planning as an obstacle. Such things as master-planning, building committees, architects and qualified builders are, in their view, obstacles to the construction of a building. They may picture good stewardship and wise financial planning as further delays to the building program. Build now and pay later is their motto.

Usually, people who want to build the building now are shortsighted. Somebody has the picture of a church building or an idea of the kind they would like. Someone in the congregation or a relative or a friend is willing to draw up some plans and someone volunteers to build the building for far less than any contractor. It seems very simple; unencumbered with troublesome details.

A third group wants to make extensive studies and plans. Feasibility studies, market analyses and surveys become their major concerns. They see borrowing money as either unwise or unbiblical, or both. Building plans are drawn. Sometimes so much time elapses before it is time to build that it is necessary to appoint a new committee. Because the new committee wasn't included in the original planning, its members may have other ideas of what kind of a building the church needs. Delays often mean increased interest rates and construction costs. By the time the building committee is ready to build, the congregation has lost interest in supporting the venture. The urgency is gone. Before discussing ways of handling the tension of seasonal obligations, there is one other type of obligation that churches face.

Immediate Obligations

When a crisis occurs in a church or in a community, it is essential to respond immediately. A family may experience a death, a serious accident, a financial setback or another kind of tragedy. This is no time for selecting a committee or making a survey or studying the situation. Although there are risks involved in responding in a wrong way, most efforts are better than no response or a late response.

The day before one of our Deacon Board meetings the roof collapsed in a new church in our city. We did not know all of the details. Some people suggested that we shouldn't act hastily. What was the extent of the damage? How much insurance did they have? Were other churches going to help? Did their denomination have a responsibility?

Although these questions were all valid, this was a time for immediate action. Eventually there might be a financial resolution to the problem. They needed immediate help and encouragement, right now. The next Sunday we shared this need with our congregation. We received an offering of over $1,400.00. I don't know whether that immediate response did more for the congregation that lost its roof, or for the congregation that gave money. Sometimes in the life of a church, just as in the life of an individual, we need to take instantaneous action o react immediately.

As we saw earlier, the writer of the book of Ecclesiastes described the need for discernment of the proper time. "There is a time for everything, and a season for every activity under heaven. . ." We need to know when to act now and when to wait until later.

The following guidelines will help us maintain a productive balance of our *now/then* tension.

Prayer

In Proverbs 16:1-3 we read, "To man belong the plans of the heart, but from the Lord comes the reply of the tongue. All a man's ways seem innocent to him, but motives are weighed by the Lord. Commit to the Lord whatever you do, and your plans will succeed." It appears that man is the one that does the planning. But verse 9 indicates that the real guidance must come from the Lord. "In his heart a man plans his course. but the Lord determines his steps."

We must make our decisions according to God's timetable. Without fervent prayer by the decision makers and the entire congregation, our timing is bound to be wrong. After the Ascension, Jesus told the disciples to wait for the coming of the Holy Spirit. During the 10-day period of waiting, they handled one item of business. They selected an apostle named Matthias to take the place of Judas. In Acts 1:23,24 we read, "So they proposed two men: Joseph called Barsabbas (also known as Justus) and Matthias. Then they prayed, 'Lord, you know everyone's heart. Show us which one of these two you have chosen. . .'" If they had waited a few more days for the coming of the Holy Spirit, He would have guided them. It's significant that we never hear of Matthias again.

Prayer is always important in the life of a church, but it is essential when choosing leaders. Without the mind of Christ and the prompting of the Holy Spirit, our decisions become carnal. Many leaders in churches are chosen on the basis of personality and ability, rather than on spirituality. Don't make that mistake.

Patience

Our picture of patience is often a distorted one. Patience is not sitting back with our arms folded, doing nothing and waiting for the inevitable to happen. In Hebrews 6:12 we read, "We do not want you to become lazy, but to imitate those who through faith and patience inherit what has been promised." We are to remain occupied until Jesus comes. Patience does not mean either procrastinating or being presumptuous. Patience is relying on the Lord's strength and waiting for His direction. God's will and God's timing are inseparable. When God says wait, we can't hurry; and when He says hurry, we can't wait. If you don't have the Lord's direction on a now/then decision, stick it out until He speaks.

Priorities

A church's leaders should constantly be examining the church's priorities in light of its objectives. Before priorities are established, clear objectives and measurable goals must be in place. Listing priorities is simply a means of deciding which goals should come first. If a new building is the number one goal, then effort and time will be given to seeing this accomplished. Roger C. Palms in his book *First Things First* comments, "There are always more demands than time to meet them: more meetings, more informal conversations, more trips, more questions to be answered, there are items to fix, family needs to care for, and people to help. Life isn't lived apart from tension. We have to do all that we do in the midst of all the interruptions, even those caused by everyone else.

"By establishing priorities, we will have to do adequately what needs to be done — to eliminate what doesn't need to be done; to know what can be postponed and what can be done by others, so that we can live our lives within a family, a community, and world that has its priorities, too."[2] Churches need to have priorities. They help determine what must be done now and what can be done later.

Church staff and boards need to establish priorities. So should committees, classes and organizations in the church. These need to be coordinated with other groups to avoid overlap and conflict. At least every couple of years the entire congregation should be involved in a prioritization process to determine the church's goals.

Process

In many areas of church life it's not a question of whether we do something now or later, but "did we go through the process of touching all the bases?" There are steps to follow, individuals to consult, committees to contact, information to be gathered and discussion to take place before a decision can be reached. The process of building, the process of discipling, the process of discipline and the process of maturation all take time.

The problem with any process in the church is that sometimes there is no conclusion or growth. It is not enough to merely increase activity. Process should result in progress. Decisions need to include a means of evaluation. Results can be measured when there are specific objectives to achieve within a set time frame. Because of the approaching return of Christ, we feel the urgency of action. But we shouldn't neglect those activities which are important.

When I was a student in college, my roommate had a sign on his desk: "As Now, So Then." As we do things now, so they will become later. The discipline, priorities, goals and objectives in a church should be established now, because they will affect the direction and destiny of the church later.

Footnotes

1. Hummel, Charles E., *Tyranny of the Urgent* (Downers Grove, IL: Inter-Varsity Press, 1967), p. 5.

2. Palms, Roger C., *First Things First* (Wheaton, IL: Victor Books, 1983), pp. 9, 10.

12

Counting Heads Or Weighing Hearts?

The Tension Between "Quantity and Quality"

My first Sunday as the new pastor of Temple Baptist Church was "Watermelon Sunday." The church is located in metropolitan Portland. Because it is a commercial area, few people live in the neighborhood. Potential for growth in the immediate area, especially among children and youth, is extremely limited.

The church launched an extensive bus program, sending out as many as nine buses into the surrounding neighborhoods. Hundreds of kids came on the buses, many hearing the gospel for the first time, in our Sunday school. Various promotional methods such as giving out coupons for hamburgers, distributing free yo-yos, etc., were used to encourage children to come.

In order to ensure a good attendance for the new preacher, "Watermelon Sunday" was planned. Every youngster who came on a bus was to receive a free watermelon. When the service began, kids were everywhere. Attendance was great. But the atmosphere of the entire service was disruptive. I barely made it through. The children who had come on the buses certainly did not worship. I doubt whether anybody did.

If this scenario represented what church growth was all about, I knew I didn't want it. In fact, the survival of my sanity, as well as my ministry, depended on finding a different approach to church growth.

Numerical growth in a church always was important to me. I liked the challenge of a Sunday school contest. Not only did I believe this was the way that churches grew, but it fed my competitive instincts. We had a Sunday school contest in the first church that I pastored. The church was divided into two groups — the red group and the green group. (We weren't very creative with names in those days.) We named the contest "Vote for Sunday School." Each Sunday, people voted for their group as they entered the church. I noticed one couple that didn't sign in. "Hey, you forgot to vote!" I hollered as they came through the doors. "We are not voting," they answered. "It's a sin to count people. David was punished for numbering the people."

The Church Growth Tension

Whether or not you agree with their answer, these people and this situation bring into focus a common tension in many churches. As the local body of Christ we struggle to choose between concentrating on producing a quantity of believers and producing a group with spiritual quality, whatever its size. Both are attempts to identify a way to measure church health and growth.

Some Christians equate large churches with being spiritual. Others equate smallness with spirituality and bigness with superficiality. This tension exists both within churches and between churches. It is not confined to any section of the country or any religious group.

Advocates of both quantity and quality in the local church look to the New Testament church to support their position. Those who say that *church growth* is measured *quantitatively*, point to the many passages where numbers of people appear to be prominent. In Acts 2:41 we read, "Those who accepted his message were baptized, and about three thousand were added to their number that day." And in Acts 2:47 we read, "And the Lord added to their number daily those who were being saved." In Acts 4:4 the emphasis again is on numerical growth: "But many who heard the message believed, and the number of men *grew* to about five thousand." In Acts 5:14, the number of new believers included women, "...more and more men and women believed in the Lord and were added to their number."

Those who say that *church growth* is measured *qualitatively* use verses such as Colossians 1:10: "And we pray this in order that you may live a life worthy of the Lord and may please him in every way: bearing fruit in every good work, *growing* in the knowledge of God..." In 2 Peter 3:18, Peter stresses growing as qualitative, "But *grow* in the grace and knowledge of our Lord and Savior Jesus Christ." Paul, in Ephesians 4:15,16, urged the believers "...in all things *grow* up into him who is the Head, that is, Christ. From him the whole body, joined and held together by every supporting ligament, *grows* and builds itself up in love, as each part does its work."

Before the tension can be adjusted between our opposite emphases on quantity and quality of disciples, we need to look at some of the wrong ways these two Biblical concepts have been applied.

Playing the Numbers Game

When I was pastoring my first church in rural Michigan, I

attended a pastors' luncheon every week with about 20 to 25 other pastors. When I first started attending these meetings, I felt inferior and conspicuous. I was pastoring a brand new church out in the country, and we were quite small in comparison to other churches. After a few meetings I discovered that the name of the game each week was the "numbers game." "How many did you have in Sunday school last week?" "What was your morning attendance last Sunday?" "How many members do you have now?" "How many kids did you have at Vacation Bible School?" "How many decisions did you have yesterday?" These were some of the questions I heard week after week. I observed that the questioner made sure that he had a good attendance in the category about which he asked. It is funny that no one ever asked how many people were in prayer meeting.

I became obsessed with numbers. On the way home we would add up the number of people we knew were in attendance. If our number exceeded the ushers' count, we substituted ours. Of course, if our number was lower than theirs, we assumed we must have made a mistake. On Sunday afternoon I would fold the chairs in the back of the church so it would appear that there were more people in the evening service because every chair was filled. The highlight of the year was the fall Sunday school contest. It was interesting to see how each church established its base number and what methods it used to draw a crowd.

One Monday I saw a man who pastored a large church in a nearby city. His first words to me were, "Fred, we had a great service last night in our church. We had a hundred decisions!" He paused for a moment and then put the statistic in perspective. "There were two for and ninety-eight against," he said. Sometimes numbers don't tell you much.

We can use numbers to prove just about anything. When I was in seminary I learned how some churches are able to use figures to paint a false picture. I took a course on the Rural Church. One of our assignments was to make a graph of the growth patterns of Baptist church associations in rural Illinois over the previous 25 years. When the project was completed, we were to report back to the class with our findings. We were amazed to discover that a familiar pattern developed in every association. All experienced a decline in membership over the 25-year period. But at the same time, churches usually showed membership gains during each pastor's tenure.

How could this happen? Actually, it was a very simple process. When a pastor is called to a new parish, the first thing he does is "prune" the rolls of all the deadwood. The figure he uses to determine the membership number at the beginning of his ministry is the "pruned" figure. When he leaves after several years, more deadwood has accumulated. The increase during his tenure at the church includes the new deadwood. When the next pastor comes, he begins by "pruning" the membership roll again. When he concludes his ministry after several years, he counts the total number of members including the deadwood that has built up again over the years since he began as pastor. Pastors showed an increase over the years, but churches did not.

Those who are connected with ecclesiastical organizations know how important numbers are. Not only are they important for completing statistical reports, but numbers play a factor in the evaluation, promotion, or relocation of members of the pastoral staff. Sometimes decisions and recommendations are based purely on quantity. One church in which I served as pastor had had tremendous numerical growth over a short period. In analyzing the membership statistics, we discovered that some of the people had been added twice, and in one case the same person had been added three times in a row. Numerical figures continue to be used as a measurement of success in most churches.

Someone has estimated that five percent of all church members don't exist and ten percent of all church members can't be found. What these statistics mean is that five percent of all church members have died and their names have never been removed from the membership lists. Second, ten percent of all church members have moved and no one in the church has any idea where they went.

The Church Obese

Not all the excesses and misapplications of biblical teaching on growth center around an emphasis on quantity and numbers. Peter Wagner describes several different diseases, one of which he calls "koinonitis." This disease comes from churches who want to grow inwardly only. They emphasize fellowship, relationships and qualitative growth, and are not interested in reaching out to the unsaved. In fact, some of the congregations consider large churches and groups as unspiritual.

When I was living in New England, we worked to start a new church. Initially, we had a few families that met for prayer and Bible study. Then we decided to hold Sunday worship services in a school. The church quickly grew in numbers. In a nearby town there was an older, established church that had experienced very little numerical growth for decades. When the members heard of the rapid growth of our church, their initial response was, "What are they doing wrong?" Maybe we were using gimmicks or compromising beliefs, they thought, or making it too easy to join our church. If we would do things right we would be small like them.

A church that is interested only in the quality of its members will eventually die. Not from stretching itself too thin, but from becoming too fat from overeating. George W. Peters in his book *A Theology of Church Growth* comments, "God does not bless the church in order to fatten it. He builds muscle quality and not fat baggage. A stalemated, non-evangelizing, non-missionary church definitely comes under the "woe to me if I do not preach the gospel," as Paul expresses it in 1 Corinthians 9:16. Sooner or later the sap will dry up in the tree, branches will wilt, wither, and dry up and death will seep down to the roots."[1]

What makes a church successful? Is it quantity or quality? Both or neither? The term "success" is one that many people connected with the church consider a bad word. I attended a church leadership conference in California. Many denominations were represented. Two sermons were scheduled for the first afternoon. The first speaker talked about the evil concept of 'success' that had infiltrated the church. His thesis was that 'success' is not a spiritual term, but a worldly term. Success is a term that relates to gaining wealth and fame. Churches are not to be successful, but faithful. His speech was billed as the keynote address for the entire week.

I felt sorry for the second speaker that afternoon. His sermon was also on the subject of success. But he believed that every church should be successful. What made matters even worse was that the first letter of each of his main points spelled out the acrostic SUCCESS.

Many Scriptures, such as Genesis 24:12 and Joshua 1:8, indicate that God's people prayed for and sought success. But note this: success is not a quantitative or qualitative term; it simply means "the satisfactory completion of something," or "a favorable or desired outcome." We measure the term success not by the amount of activity that is taking place, but by the results that are achieved.

Two Sides of the Same Coin

Does God count heads or weigh hearts? Does it matter what

kind of growth we are experiencing as long as we are growing? Can we measure growth?

Both quantity and quality are biblical concepts. In fact, they are different sides of the same coin. Although we must distinguish between the opposite aspects of quantity and quality, they should not be separated.

Both aspects are essential. If we want lasting growth, it must be biblical growth. Christian organizations that want to grow should realize that healthy growth takes place in a proper environment. The apostle Paul gives us a good guideline for healthy growth, in 1 Corinthians 3:5-8, "...the Lord has assigned to each his task. I planted the seed, Apollos watered it, but God made it grow. So neither he who plants nor he who waters is anything, but only God, who makes things grow. The man who plants and the man who waters have one purpose..."

The church is an organism. If it is to have healthy growth, it will result from planting, watering and fertilizing. That is our work. God will cause the increase. The basic word for growth in the New Testament is not used in a quantitative sense, but in a qualitative one. Donald Roberts in his book *The Perfect Church* comments that "We need to be aware of...cliche formulas for church growth which equate success with methods, men and multitudes of people."[2]

Growth is from God. Paul pictures the process as similar to the construction of a building. In Ephesians 2:19-22 we are described as "...members of God's household, built on the foundation of the apostles and prophets, with Christ Jesus himself as the chief cornerstone. In him the whole building is joined together and rises to become a holy temple in the Lord. And in him you too are being built together to become a dwelling in which God lives by his Spirit." In Matthew 16:18 Jesus told Peter, "...I will build my church, and the gates of Hades will not overcome it."

A Quality Community

Many people equate this building process with numerical increase and geographical expansion. In the New Testament, the basic meaning of building is construction or development. Before a church can increase numerically or expand geographically, it must be built up. The church is a quality community because its members are the dwelling place of the Holy Spirit.

What are the attributes of a quality church? Dr. George W. Peters, professor at Dallas Theological Seminary, lists nine:

1. A church must experientially know the presence of the Holy Spirit
2. A church must be united by a common faith
3. A church must submit itself to a God-ordained leadership
4. A church must be molded into a unified, functioning community
5. A church must train its members in the school of discipleship
6. A church must proclaim a clearly defined and relevant message
7. A church must continue in prayer
8. A church must live in the realm of miracles
9. A church must suffer and sacrifice joyfully.[3]

The objectives of a growing church are worship, edification and evangelism. Quality in achieving these objectives is not an end in itself. Biblical quality results in numerical growth, which in turn is developed into additional quality.

This was the pattern in the New Testament Church. In Acts 9:31,32 we read that ". . . the church . . . was *strengthened;* and *encouraged* by the Holy Spirit, it *grew in numbers,* living in the fear of the Lord." In Acts 11:22-24 Barnabas was sent to Antioch. "When he arrived and saw the *evidence of the grace of God,* he was glad and encouraged them all to remain true to the Lord with all their hearts...and a *great number of people* were brought to the Lord." Barnabas came back to Antioch with Paul for a whole year. Together, they spent their time teaching the large number who believed in the Lord.

A Strategy for Balance

Although centuries have passed, methods have changed and new cultures have emerged, growth principles and tensions have remained the same. There are still people who want to substitute numbers for excellence in the local church and others who emphasize quality to the exclusion of numerical growth. Neither aspect of church growth is to be sacrificed for the other. The principle of balance between quality and quantity is more than a principle. It is a strategy for growth in the local church.

Here are some steps and guidelines that will help you determine if your church has accomplished a healthy balance between quality and numerical growth.

1. *Decide on the Purpose of Growth*
The purpose of the church, both universally and locally, is to glorify God. An ad on television proclaimed the purpose of one company in in the following way: "We don't want to be the biggest, we just want to be the best." To achieve a proper balance between quality and quantity, our emphasis should be on making of disciples, not on counting the number of decisions.

God has used evangelists throughout the years to preach the message of salvation to large numbers of people. Many testify that they began the Christian life one night at a great evangelistic crusade. The problem with crusades is not that the message is unclear, or even that the method is incorrect, but that many Christians do not understand the purpose of the meetings.

Usually, after the evangelistic meetings, a record is kept of the decisions made. Sometimes the numbers are based on how many people came forward or how many people signed a decision card. Neither is a true barometer. Some of us may have taken part in the "I Found It" campaign in various cities in the United States. Many people signed decision cards, but never became disciples. It seems to me that only those who had previously had a meaningful relationship with other believers were able to continue the process of growth.

Discipling is a process that brings the gospel message to people, leading them to make a commitment to the Lord Jesus Christ, seeing them baptized, uniting with a local church, training them and encouraging them to reach others for Christ. Matthew 28:18-20 gives us both a purpose and the plan for achieving that purpose.

2. Define the Kinds of Growth
A. Biological Growth

Membership additions to local churches come in three basic ways—biological growth (converts of church members' children), transfer growth and kingdom growth (new converts). One of the greatest experiences in the life of a church is to see children and grandchildren of church members make a commitment to Christ. As they grow and mature they find places of Christian service both within and outside the local church structures. Churches and parents should see the great opportunity and great responsibility they have to reproduce their Christian faith in their children.

B. Transfer Growth

Much reported church growth is caused by people changing churches. Some people shift from church to church because they are socially or vocationally mobile. Moving from place to place necessitates changing churches.

Another kind of transfer growth results from people within

a community who constantly are "church shopping." People appear to wander from church to church for two basic reasons. The first is that they are seeking entertainment. These are the people who show up at the church almost every time we have an exciting speaker or program. Secondly, people travel from church to church in order to keep from making a commitment and becoming involved. For some reason, these people desire anonymity.

When we talk about people transferring their church membership, the subject of "sheep stealing" usually comes up. In over 25 years of ministry I have seen only a couple of instances which even remotely fit that description. You can't steal well-fed sheep. Rev. John Garlington, former pastor of Maranatha Church in Portland, Oregon, described "sheep stealing" from his perspective. "We have a high fence around our church. In some places there are small holes in the fence. There are some skinny sheep that walk around the fence and they crawl through the holes. When they come to our church, we fatten them up and they can't get back through the holes."

C. Kingdom Growth

The third kind of growth is conversion growth or kingdom growth. This kind of growth comes from church members reaching the lost for Christ. Usually, conversion growth is a result of church members sharing their faith with people whom they already know, such as relatives, friends, neighbors, classmates and business associates. Local church leaders should analyze church growth statistics. Biological growth is important, but if this is the only kind, a church will become ingrown and stagnant.

If the major growth in your church is by transferring people, your church probably does not emphasize evangelism. Kingdom growth indicates that the church members are taking the Great Commission as a personal and group responsibility. The process of discipleship has already begun. All three kinds of growth — biological, transfer and kingdom growth — are important. But the major growth in churches should be kingdom growth.

3. *Declare the Decision to Grow*

Growth comes about in two ways — one is very natural. A church that is concerned about the nurture and training of each believer will experience not only qualitative growth, but also quantitative growth. Churches, like plants, will grow organically if the proper environment is maintained. It's essential that a church provide a growth climate for its members.

The conscious decision to grow, however, should also include a place for intentional growth. Some churches do not plan to grow. Even though growth results from maintaining a proper environment, it is not automatic. Quantity cannot become an excuse for lack of quality. Dr. George Peters comments, "In the Western world where quantity is difficult to achieve, churches are quick in excusing themselves by saying that they prefer a membership of quality. The reasoning is that if quality is accomplished, quantity will naturally result. Ideologically, this sounds logical and appealing. Practically, this does not match reality. It may be more rationalization than honest admission of some basic weakness and/or failure."[4]

Growth is often spontaneous. It should also be planned. When your church makes intentional growth plans, your pastoral staff, the governing body of your church and your congregation are part of the decision making process. Publicize your decision and the goals that result from it so that everyone understands the church's direction. Use the pulpit and other communication tools to get out your message.

4. *Develop the Process of Growth*

Each church is unique. One danger to avoid is that of trying to adopt another church's program. What works in one place may not work in another. When Temple Baptist Church embarked on a bus ministry, we tried to copy a very large church's program from a different sociological and geographical setting. The people at Temple were not a part of the decision making process or implementation of the ministry. As a result, our efforts were less effective.

This does not mean that your church should develop its own church growth materials. Many good programs are available, such as Navigators, Churches Alive, Evangelism Explosion and Way of Life. But all materials will be more applicable when they are adapted to your local situation.

Whatever emphasis your church uses to achieve quantitative growth, it must not overshadow or overpower qualitative growth. At the height of our bus ministry at Temple Baptist Church, 80% of the people in our Sunday school were coming on the buses, while 20% of those attending were trying to maintain the programs as well as provide teaching. The teaching was strong, but the number of teachers were few. There was no way that so many people could effectively be assimilated into the life of the church at one time. Although most churches have the opposite problem — too few outsiders attending the church — a proper balance must be maintained between quantity and quality.

5. *Determine the Obstacles to Church Growth*

Obstacles to church growth can come from either external or internal sources. Quantitative growth can be hampered when a town or region has too many churches or too few people. In some rural areas, where the population is minimal or there has been a large exodus of people, churches may find it difficult to experience any significant growth.

In other places where the gospel is presented, you may run into great resistance. We have been conditioned to believe that people will be receptive if we preach the gospel. This is not always true. In areas where other religions and cults have permeated a large percentage of the population, it becomes extremely difficult for a church to add people to its membership at a healthy rate. In such cases, local churches can be aggressive in planting churches in other locations as well as in trying to reach those nearby.

When people within the local church resist reaching out, this presents a different challenge. If the present leaders are opposed to reaching new people in their community, new leaders must be sought and trained.

6. *Design the Measurements of Growth*

It is fairly simple to measure statistical growth. Charts, graphs and diagrams can measure all types of attendance and giving statistics. It's much more difficult, however, to measure qualitative growth. But there are several ways to determine if the body is being built up as well as getting larger. In Ephesians 4:13, Paul talks about the building up of the body as we "... reach unity in the faith and in the knowledge of the Son of God and become mature..." Maturity is not determined by growing older or larger, but by growing up.

Whether or not a church is growing in maturity can be measured in several ways. One way to measure maturity is to evaluate the hunger and thirst of the congregation for righteousness. Another way is to determine the number of people who are involved in growth experiences between Sundays, such as Bible studies, care groups, growth groups, cell groups, etc.

Answering the following questions will tell you much about the health and maturity of your church. Are people exhibiting the fruit of the Spirit found in Galatians 5:22,23: "... love, joy, peace, patience, kindness, goodness, faithfulness, gentleness, and self-control"? Is there an indication of family solidarity in the church? Are families staying together and loving each other as well? Is there a formal or informal discipling process taking place?

Sometimes qualitative growth can be seen in little things. Do the people really enjoy one another? In one church in New England where I spoke, I noticed that five minutes after the benediction no cars were left in the parking lot. An indicator of growth not only may be seen by how people worship together, but in how they have fellowship together.

A healthy church is both maturing and multiplying. God not only weighs hearts, but counts heads. We need a balance between quantity and quality in our churches. It won't just happen by itself. Our environment for growth must be maintained and we must pursue an intentional purpose to disciple people by reaching, preaching and teaching.

Footnotes

1. Peters, George W., *A Theology of Church Growth* (Grand Rapids, MI: Zondervan, 1981), p. 192.
2. Roberts, Donald, *The Perfect Church* (Harrisburg, PA: Christian Publications, Inc., 1974), p. 51.
3. *Op.Cit.*, Peters, p. 139.
4. *Ibid.*, p. 191.

13

Help Wanted: Tension Adjusters

My brother was an active person all his life. He held two jobs. His full-time job was as school teacher. Although this kept him mentally and emotionally active, it wasn't physically demanding. His part-time job was being a mailman. Handling mail bags, sorting letters and delivering mail gave him plenty of physical exercise.

His family was shocked when he was rushed to the hospital for by-pass heart surgery. In fact, he had five by-passes. Following the surgery, the doctor said that the only thing that had kept my brother alive was his exercise bike. Over the years he had ridden over 75,000 miles on his stationary bike. Even though his arteries were almost entirely clogged, he was otherwise in good physical condition.

One sophisticated exercise bike is called a Lifecycle. It is unique in that the resistance of the pedals is controlled directly by a planned personal program regulated by computer. Each person sets his or her own program based on the time he has available to spend on the cycle and the intensity of exercise which he can handle. If there is no tension on the pedals, the person keeps spinning around and accomplishes nothing. If there is too much tension, the value of the exercise is diminished and the rider may collapse of exhaustion.

Churches resemble these Lifecycles in several ways. Neither exercise cycles nor churches run by themselves. No matter how nice they look or how well they are built, they need people to help them function. Each cycle and each church is unique. Although the basic needs of the people that use them are the same, they need individual adjustment if they are to be of maximum benefit to the users.

Some churches have no stated purpose, no objectives and no measurable goals. They are involved in a plethora of activities but are accomplishing little. Instead of measuring results, people are measuring activities. In some ways this is like the rider on the exercycle who spins the pedals, but the chain isn't hooked up.

Other churches are not making progress because a myriad of tensions are constantly sapping their vitality. Every time someone suggests a plan of action, someone counters it with a different plan of action. Like the pedals of the exercycle, nothing is accomplished because the amount of friction restricts any forward movement. People appear to be going in different directions. Someone may suggest a type of program that has been successful in another church. When it doesn't work the same way in his or her church, people become frustrated, bored, angry, guilty or indifferent.

Every church faces the same basic tensions. It doesn't matter if the church is new or old, located in the city or in the country, affluent or poor, independent or affiliated with an ecclesiastical group. What all churches need are tension adjusters. A tension adjuster is one who is able to bring opposing forces, ideas, emphases that are opposite, into a proper balance.

Tension is vital to any church that is alive. Where there is no tension there may be commotion, but there is no forward motion. Where there is too much tension, a church can become severely handicapped or paralyzed in its pursuit of biblical objectives.

Who Is a Tension Adjuster?

Every church needs tension adjusters. Not just one or two, but a host of people who want to be used by God to help their local church to go forward. The position of tension adjuster is not an exclusive one. It is open to men or women, young or old, rich or poor. The only qualifications are that the person be spiritually mature, possess the gifts of discernment and encouragement, and be available to serve the Lord and the local church. It is essential that this person be committed to the Head of the Church and to members of the body.

A man by the name of Apollos was an effective tension adjuster in the New Testament church. Acts 18:24-28 describes the man and his ministry. Apollos was a person who was willing to learn. He had a "thorough knowledge of the Scriptures." It is essential for a person who is a "tension adjuster" to know the Word of God. Not only did Apollos know the Scriptures, but he was enthusiastic and willing to take a stand for what he believed. In verse 25 we read that he "spoke with great fervor," and in verse 26 that he spoke "boldly." He used the Scriptures both "accurately" and "vigorously."

Another basic trait that is essential to being a tension adjuster is willingness to listen and to learn. Apollos had this trait. Priscilla and Aquilla were able to instruct him. This teachable spirit is essential. His ministry was a helping one. When he arrived in Achaia, ". . .he was a great help to those who by grace had believed."

Finally, in 1 Corinthians 3:4-9 and 16:12 we read that Apollos was not willing to become the center of a controversy between himself and the Apostle Paul. His was a healing ministry, not a devisive one. His ability to relate, facilitate and communicate helped the early church to adjust its tensions so it could grow.

7 Causes of Tension

A theological and an ecclesiastical background are helpful in becoming a tension adjuster, but they are not essential. What is essential, however, is an understanding of the causes of tension. An ignorance of the causes will lead us to continual frustration and eventual paralysis of any ability we may have to adjust tensions. In the preceding chapters I have discussed the tensions that most churches experience to a greater or lesser degree at some time in their history. You may have discovered several others. Tensions themselves may change from century to century, from generation to generation and from place to place. But the basic causes remain the same. There are at least seven causes of tension in churches.

1. *Cultural Differences.* The cultural differences between Gentile believers and Jewish believers are well documented in the New Testament. Believers were conditioned by both the Greeks and the Romans. Cultural differences may or may not be related to geography. Sometimes the differences are more easily identified along racial and ethnic lines.

When I preached in the Philippines, the 8:00 p.m. service usually started at 8:45 p.m. If the service was that late in Portland, the entire congregation would be gone. The difference is not simply a geographic one. In Japan the church service starts exactly on schedule, as do the trains. On the other hand, when I preach at predominately black churches, the starting and finishing time of a worship service are not considered important.

The reason for this difference has to do with two different perspectives on time. Some cultures view time from a linear perspective. Time is seen as a straight line. Time marches on! If you miss a meeting, an appointment or an opportunity, you will never get it back. You can't stop the sundial or the digital watch from moving forward.

On the other hand, other cultures view time from a cyclical perspective. Time goes in cycles. Seasons of the year come and go, but they always return next year. If you miss something today or this week, there always is tomorrow or next week. If you don't plant this spring, you can wait until next spring.

If everybody in a local church had the same perspective on time, it would deflate some tensions. Usually this doesn't happen — you get a mix of both perspectives. Tensions also arise from people's views of life and life styles.

2. *Generational Differences.* When I was young we used to sing a little song every time we saw a funeral procession. One of the lines was, "Did you ever think as the hearse went by, that you might be the next to die?" I don't know if my parents ever sang that song, but I recently observed that now that I am a grandparent, no one my age is singing it. The reason we don't is that we now realize that it may be true. We may be the next to die. When I was young, I knew that my grandparents, parents, uncles and aunts hadn't died, so I still had plenty of time before it was my turn.

Generational differences affect our view of death. They also affect how we face life. Anyone who has been on a church board or committee knows what an impact the Great Depression of the early 1930s has on financial decisions. Those who have lost their job, depend on food stamps, or have been in a food line are usually quite conservative when it comes to participating in financial ventures they consider risky.

On the other hand, individuals who attended college or were

in Vietnam during the 1960s have had a different mark placed upon their lives. Their view of patriotism and institutionalism may be quite different from that of their parents. Our values systems are a product of our cultural milieu and the impact of historical events.

3. *Leadership Differences.* In 1 Corinthians 3 we read about a tension in the Corinthian church which was caused by differences in leadership. Maybe the cause was really a problem among believers. There were obviously many differences between Paul and Apollos. Some of these differences may have related to their personalities. Others may have been caused by their leadership styles.

Some people respond to dictatorial-style leaders, while others feel more comfortable with a more participatory style of leader. Some leaders get things accomplished by demanding, while others rely on demonstrating.

An effective leader, no matter what his personality or style, will be in front of his people. If, however, he or she gets too far ahead, he will be perceived as the enemy.

4. *Theological Differences.* Quite often we deal with issues that result from differences in interpreting the Scripture. Not everyone has been to seminary and had a course in hermeneutics (the study of biblical interpretation). Although almost all Protestant churches claim the Bible as their authority, it is amazing how many differences appear. Some of these differences relate to the interpretation of basic doctrines. Teachings about the ministry of the Holy Spirit, methods of baptism, forms of worship and kinds of church organization quite often result in both tension and conflict.

The first questions that some people ask when they visit a new church shows the importance that they place on theological differences. Some of these questions are: "What do you believe about tithing?" "What do you believe about women in the ministry?" "Do you support Billy Graham?" "What is your position on the rapture?" "Do you use the King James Version of the Bible?" "What is your view of the charismatic movement?" Many of these questions can become the subject of theological debate and discussion. Some also have become the fuel that has led to an explosion.

5. *Spiritual Differences.* In 1 Corinthians 2 and 3, Paul identifies three categories of people. All three are in the church: the man without the Holy Spirit, the spiritual man and the worldly man. Differences in spiritual maturity, or lack of it, are a continued source of tension. Although quite often spiritual maturity corresponds to the length of time that a person has been a Christian, it is also possible to grow older without growing up.

The church is not a club for the spiritually mature. Its doors are open wide to all. We need to recognize, however, the difficulties that churches face when immature people are placed in leadership.

6. *Personal Preference.* For a year we served dinner every Wednesday night at church. Some people would not come unless they knew what was on the menu each week. Today, more than ever, people are nutrition and diet conscious. It is not only on Wednesday night dinners that people are concerned about their food. Some people want a steady diet of the "old-fashioned" hymns, while others want a constant supply of "praise choruses." Some prefer the lecture method of teaching, while others want only the discussion method.

Most of us are products of our ecclesiastical backgrounds. Some of us want to perpetuate our ecclesiastical heritage. Others react strongly against their past experiences of worship and structure. Some people's preferences remain static throughout their lifetime, while others learn to experience and acquire new tastes.

7. *Priorities.* Lloyd Dahlquist, former Executive Secretary

of the Baptist General Conference, commented on several occasions that "Life is measured by its priorities." For the most part, the activities in the majority of churches are good ones. The problem is that they are either out of balance or have become a substitute for the best things. There are many agendas in the local church — some hidden and some very open. People's pet projects and areas of concern run into conflict with other people's pet projects and areas of concern. Missions, music, youth, evangelism, fellowship, Sunday school, Women's Ministry, social ministry, or the building program become the main, and sometimes the only, area of interest. Sometimes a person's area of interest and expertise becomes such an obsession that it overshadows all other activities in the church.

Causes of tension may not always be easy to identify. Sometimes there may be more than one cause. In the case of my hat there were generational differences, cultural differences, spiritual differences, leadership differences and some differences of personal preference. Tensions may surface in many ways. Wise leaders in a church will be aware of the causes, not only so they can identify them, but so they can keep these forces in proper balance.

Qualities of Tension Adjusters

Recognizing causes is only part of the process. A tension adjuster is one who possesses certain qualifications that enable him or her to do what others are unable to unwilling to do. There are five qualities that tension adjusters possess. As you read on, consider how well you fit these descriptions.

1. *They Are Healthy People.*

A healthy person is one who produces, promotes and maintains wholeness. A check of his spiritual vital signs will indicate his commitment to the Lord, the Head of the Church, and to the body. Personal qualities such as discipline, purity, generosity, honesty and humility should be evident. Not only is he spiritually healthy, but a tension adjuster has a great desire to do whatever is necessary to prevent disease in a church.

Many institutions are infected because they thought that they were immune to disease. Satan is not chained. He is constantly trying to disrupt the unity of the church. Tension adjusters are concerned about personal spiritual health. They are also vigilant in protecting the church against the infiltration of the enemy.

2. *They Are Balanced People.*

A tension adjuster is a team player. Some people excel in activities that demand individual effort. The church, however, is a body and therefore its members function together with others. Teamwork means the subordination of personal prominence so that the whole body may function efficiently. An ability to have a proper perspective of the whole body is necessary to maintain balance in a church. If a tension adjuster is not a balanced person in his or her own life, he will have trouble trying to maintain equilibrium in the church. A person who is an extremist in his or her views or actions will find it difficult to maintain a proper balance in the church.

3. *They Are Growing People.*

A tension adjuster is not content with the status quo. He or she is open to new ideas, new methods and new approaches. He has a desire to see the church develop toward maturity. Activity in itself is not sufficient, but he desires to be productive in light of mutual goals. A growing person is one who enjoys variety, is willing to take risks and is open to suggestions and criticism.

4. *They Are Stretching People.*

In Philippians 3:13,14 Paul tells the church, "...One thing I do: Forgetting what is behind and straining toward what is ahead, I press on toward the goal..." A tension adjuster does not give up easily. He or she is willing to "go the second mile," and make every effort to see that the church achieves its objectives. Stretching causes people to reach farther. By stretching, a church can accomplish more than it thought was possible. Stretching the muscles allows a church to bend, but not break.

5. *They Are Optimistic People.*

Some people are always telling everyone why things in a church won't work. A tension adjuster looks at obstacles as opportunities. There are difficult people and ornery people, but none are impossible. Situations are challenges, not obstacles. A tension adjuster is a person of vision, but not an unrealistic visionary.

Meet Evelyn Smith: Tension Adjuster

The most effective tension adjuster I have ever known is a woman who is a widow in her seventies. She has no theological training. She does not hold any office in the church. She is an uncommon person with a common name — Evelyn Smith. She possesses all the qualifications that an effective tension adjuster needs. I can think of no specific instance or heroic act that qualifies her as a tension adjuster. But tension adjustment is her way of life.

Evelyn is a healthy person, spiritually. Her commitment to the Lord, to the body, and to the leadership of the church is without question. Although she understands that there are tensions in the church, she is committed to being part of the healing process. A tension adjuster must be a prayer warrior. Whenever there is a regular prayer service or a special prayer meeting she is present. She not only prays, but believes in answers to prayer.

Her approach to ministry is balanced both within and outside the church. Her ministry is not confined to one age or to one location. On a regular basis she helps at the church day care center and tutors at the public school. During the summer she spends a month working at the church camp. She also spends time helping at the retirement home associated with the church, and serves hot meals to the elderly in the community.

A balanced ministry as a tension adjuster must not be locked into the status quo, but must be a growing one. A concern of Evelyn's is the assimilation of new people into our church. When she meets new people she makes herself acquainted and then follows up these contacts with phone calls and visits. When a person leaves the church either temporarily or permanently, Evelyn continues to communicate with him by mail. Each year she writes hundreds of letters to missionaries, college students and to people in the military. She shares information about these people with the church staff and congregation. Her sense of anticipation is amazing. People in the hospital and in nursing homes receive visits from Evelyn before most people know there is a need.

Most people want to work in areas in which they are comfortable. Evelyn is stretching herself into new areas. Whenever there is a need for volunteers, she is ready to help. She helps in the office collating pages for reports and tabulating surveys or making phone calls. Even without being asked, she volunteers to do such things as putting the inserts in the bulletin on Sunday, and collecting money for the church dinners on Wednesday nights. For several years she volunteered to assist with the bus ministry in whatever way she could.

There is a danger when a person is always stretching himself/herself. Personally, someone can only stretch so far. Anyone involved in the tension process must be careful to release the tension occasionally. Twice a year Evelyn goes to a house on the coast so that she can be renewed in body and spirit. Being a tension adjuster, although it is rewarding work, is hard work.

Whether there is a need for teachers, a need for finances, or personal needs, Evelyn remains optimistic. When the church sets goals she is always optimistic that we will reach our objectives. Her personal encouraging support of the leadership in our church is invaluable. I have received dozens of cards and letters over the years from Evelyn. Many times after a long day, a discouraging experience or upon returning from a trip, I have found a letter from Evelyn in my mail box.

Exciting Days for Tension Adjusters

Everyone cannot be an Evelyn Smith. She is a unique person with unique gifts. But everyone can do his or her part to adjust the tensions in the church.

We need to recognize the difference between healthy and unhealthy tension in the church. Satan will use tension to undermine the unity and purity of the church. As the problems in the world and in the community increase, so do the problems that the church faces. The church is not only under attack from outside, but also at times from within. There is pressure to lower the moral standards and to compromise biblical beliefs. There are those who want to take shortcuts and to abandon the pursuit of excellence in the church.

These are exciting days. Not only are the last days characterized by evil, but also by opportunity. Of all the times in history, these are the most challenging. In every church we need people to creatively help adjust tensions. People in churches like yours and mine. People like Evelyn Smith. People like you.